DESTINY

WHAT'S LIFE ALL ABOUT?

KRISH KANDIAH

MONARCH
BOOKS

Oxford, UK & Grand Rapids, Michigan, USA

First published in the UK in 2007 by Monarch Books (a publishing imprint of Lion Hudson plc), Wilkinson House, Jordan Hill Road, Oxford, OX2 8DR.
Tel: +44 (0) 1865 302750   Fax: +44 (0) 1865 302757
Email: monarch@lionhudson.com
www.lionhudson.com

ISBN: 978-1-85424-846-6 (UK)
ISBN: 978-0-8254-6180-4 (USA)

Distributed by:
UK: Marston Book Services Ltd, PO Box 269, Abingdon, Oxon OX14 4YN;
USA: Kregel Publications, PO Box 2607, Grand Rapids, Michigan 49501.

Cover image by Ventileit care of www.sxc.hu
Photographs by Jonathan Self, Roger Chouler, Estelle Lobban and Julia Mosca

British Library Cataloguing Data
A catalogue record for this book is available from the British Library.

Printed and bound in Malta by Gutenberg Press.

Contents

fast-forward.rewind.pause

If life were a DVD, I would have spent most of mine holding down the fast-forward button. When I was four I wanted to go to school; when I was at school I wanted to be at college; when I was at college I wanted to be at university, and when I got to university I was itching to get stuck into a paid job. Now I am pressing fast-forward as I look forward to paying off my mortgage and taking early retirement. The future always seems better and more fun than the present, and I can't wait to get there. Is the best part of a DVD the ending?

However, when I walk down the street with my young daughter skipping along beside me, someone always stops me to say: "Make the most of it while it lasts. I wish my kids were that small again..." It seems that the older we get, it's not the fast-forward button we want to press but the rewind button. Our grandparents love to tell us the stories of their youth: the first time they met each other, what happened on the day of their wedding, what their first house was like. They treasure their memories like photos in an album and they lovingly and carefully replay every moment in slow motion. I too tell my children stories from my childhood and recount some of my fondest memories. Thinking about it, perhaps all the fun has already happened, and the best part of the DVD was the opening sequence.

Whether we are fast-forward or rewind types, we all want to get the most out of life. We strive to achieve and to move onwards and upwards, or we try to settle down and feel at home, or we simply aim to remember and to pass on those memories.

This book looks at some of the common questions we wrestle with as we try to make the most of our lives. We will follow clues from DVDs I've watched but also take cues from the big story that the Christian faith provides for making sense of life. But don't worry! I won't assume that you have seen any of the films or read any part of the Bible. We will press the pause button in life as we review the plot so far and anticipate the grand finale, and work out how we get there from here.

1

Who shall I be today?

He was barely alive, floating unconscious in the raging seas. When a fishing trawler picked him up it became apparent that he had been shot several times. When he eventually came to, it was as if his brain had been reformatted. He had no intact memories at all. The only clue to his identity was a thumbnail-sized laser device embedded under his skin. When it was activated it projected a ten-digit number onto the nearest surface. The number led the amnesiac to a safety deposit box in a Swiss bank. This is the scenario that kicks off both a best-selling series of novels and the best espionage film series so far this millennium, The Bourne Identity.[1]

Maybe we can identify a little with the amnesiac struggling to find out who he really is. Many of us struggle to know who we are. As a generation we have very little memory. Certainly many of us do not look to the past to understand our identity. Most of us do not seek advice from our parents or grandparents for answers to life's questions. Our family's name, tradition and beliefs have very little impact on the decisions we make. We want to forge our own way.

Back in The Bourne Identity, the amnesiac is faced with a dilemma. He finally makes it to his Swiss bank and opens his safety deposit box. Inside are numerous passports, driving licences, fake IDs and bank account details. At this point in the movie the lead character can take his pick of the identities he has in front of him. Does he want to be an American investment banker, an English journalist with a home in a leafy suburb, or a German art critic? His identity is in his own hands.

We live in a time of incredible choice; some would say hyper-choice. This struck home when I came back from living in Albania. There, our local supermarket would have fitted inside a small shed. In actual fact it was a small shed! Mr Ramese had very little stock. But he did have one example of almost everything you could get in the country. There was one type of bread, one kind of ketchup, one kind of jam, one kind of milk. When I returned to England I experienced culture shock merely trying to buy a hot drink.

Starbucks had arrived. I ventured in and asked for a coffee. The "barista" explained to me the options with all their different possible permutations. I could have an espresso, a latte or a mocha in a thimble-sized cup, a fat cup, a tall cup, a china cup or a cardboard cup. I could have hot milk, warm milk, frothy milk, full-fat milk, semi-skimmed milk, or milk with no fat. I thought she liked me when she began to offer me all sorts of extras. Would you like some cake with that? Some cream on top? Some marshmallows to go on the cream? Some chocolate on top of the marshmallows that are on the cream which is on the frothy milk which is on your medium-sized café latte in a cardboard cup? Then I got the bill and realized she wasn't being generous at all! We have a culture that adores choice. And it allows us to choose almost anything. We can even choose who we want to be.

This is a unique opportunity. We have a greater degree of choice about who we are than at any time in history. In previous generations, if we were born into a peasant family that was what we were and that was what we were going to stay. Identity was simple and static. It was assigned by our family's heritage, class and geography. Even our career was mapped out before we were born. We would have worked the land that had been in our family for generations, carried on the family business and maintained the family tradition.

Now there are a myriad of possibilities for who we can be. Like our coffee, our identities come with a multitude of permutations. We can be a British Asian Gothic Marxist Computer Analyst or a Lesbian Self-Employed Progressive Neo-Conservative Environmentalist. You choose. We can make decisions about our education, our careers, our marital status, our place of residence and our sexuality.

Erik Sprague grew up in a stable family. He went through the American education system and studied philosophy, graduating at the top of his class. He then embarked on a PhD. At the same time his passion for the visual arts led him to experiment with body art, tattoos and piercing. He believed his body was the ultimate canvas, and could be modified in any way that he chose. Erik chose to have his teeth sharpened, his face surgically altered and his tongue, in a major operation, forked. Erik chose who he wanted to be. He chose to be a lizard! Erik, by becoming the "lizard-man"[2], blatantly expressed his ability to choose.

We might not take it as far as Sprague. But we do seek to construct our identities to some degree. Advertisers are quick to capitalize on this. They no longer bother giving us information about the product they want us to buy. They just play some inspiring music and show a celebrity using the product, and somehow we're hooked. They know they are selling us an identity. They tell us we can be Brad Pitt just by changing our brand of razor. They tell us we can be Kate Moss by purchasing a particular eyeliner. We buy into it. If we want to be seen as discerning, we buy a quietly understated BMW. If we want a streetwise image, we get a tattoo. If we want to be known as subversive, we pick up a pair of cool anti-fit jeans. We construct our identity based on the designer label.

The iPod was a piece of marketing genius on the part of the electronics lifestyle engineers at Apple. Because they made the headphones white, everyone knew that there was an iPod on the other end of the cable in the coat pocket. The Metropolitan Police advised iPod owners in London to use black headphones because it made them less of a target for robbers. But in vain. It seems it was worth the risk of being mugged just to be seen with the unmistakable designer label of an iPod. Consumer identity and brand loyalty was more important than personal security. Someone has even written a book about this, called *ipod, therefore I am*.[3]

"Branding" is an ironic term. "Branding" used to refer to the way that slaves were marked by their owners. Now, one of the ultimate expressions of human freedom is to choose to sport a branded piece of clothing or technology. However, rather than branded clothing demonstrating what we own, we are actually showing who owns us. Although we think we are the ones with consumer choice, we are strongly influenced by media-constructed realities. We are actually living examples of the success of the marketeers. In many ways even our idea of success is shaped by the desires of multinational companies to make ever more money at our expense.

But choice is not everything. Bourne the amnesiac, rifling through his safety deposit box, does not want to know who he could be. He is not content to adopt one of the range of personas presented to him. What he wants to know is who he really is. He does not ask, "Who shall I be today?" but "Who am I really?" He wants to know the truth. He believes there is a truth to be found, and is not content until he finds it. We may enjoy choosing who we could be, but how can we possibly discover the truth about who we really are? At some point in our lives we all must face this question. Beneath the media-influenced images, behind the designer labels, beyond the desire to keep up appearances, who am I really?

Am I more than a puppet of the marketing gurus? Am I more than the projection of success I try to give out at work? Am I more than "arm candy" for my partner? At some point, to be able to live authentically in our fast-changing world, we need to know who we really are. Otherwise, whether we realize it or not, other people's agendas will continue to shape our destinies.

There are three persistent views that people hold today when they consider the issue of identity. The first is a definition that is materialistic and to do with our chemical composition. The second is a definition that is psychological and to do with our memories. The third is a definition that is sociological and to do with our relationships. Let's look briefly at each of these.

A Life Less Ordinary

You have probably heard that the average human body contains enough iron to make a three-inch nail, enough sulphur to kill all the fleas on an average dog, enough carbon to make 900 pencils, enough potassium to fire a toy cannon, enough fat to make seven bars of soap, enough phosphorous to make 2,200 match heads, and enough water to fill a ten-gallon tank. Although these facts may earn you fifteen seconds of interest at a dinner party, they are also slightly depressing. This is hardly expensive stuff! Is that all we are? Odds and ends from the garden shed?

Some people believe that we can be defined in terms of a collection of chemicals. However, to define human beings like this is as reductionist as describing a Shakespearean sonnet as a bunch of letters, or a van Gogh masterpiece as a pile of paint. The fact that there has been deliberate care and design to produce beauty makes all the difference.

"ipod therefore I am"

D. Jones

Memento

A man sits on a bench and the grim reaper creeps up behind him. Far above, removal men inadvertently drop a piano from the top floor of a block of flats. The man's whole life flashes before his eyes. The bulk of this flashback is taken up by a recent holiday (the brand of which "subtly" appears emblazoned across the screen). This holiday had obviously involved jet skiing, drinking, lots of very friendly female company, drinking, sunbathing (whilst drinking), and copious amounts of drinking! The moral of the ad is that life is short and death is an ever-present reality - but as long as you have filled your short time with memorable experiences your life is meaningful.

The concept that life is ultimately about collecting memories is not as outrageous as it appears. Medics tell us that, due to an inbuilt self-destruct mechanism in human DNA, all our cells die out and are replaced in a series of six-year periods. So in what sense are you the same person that you were six years ago?

Some thinkers argue that it is the persistence of memory that overrides the biological recycling that takes place in our bodies. They say memories make us more than chemistry, and our ability to recall is the key to our human identity. If this is true, then the constant pursuit of new exhilarating experiences does not sound so ridiculous. It will make the final flashback of our life memories more exciting. Many of us live as if this were true. We are experience junkies and we are keen to define ourselves by the sensory thrills we can collect in life. We buy tour T-shirts from live gigs, collect stamps in our passport, and immortalize moments by recording them on our camcorders and digital cameras. What is depressing is that most of us will lose our memories as we age. The irony is that we spend a

*"The centre of me is always and eternally a terrible pain –
a curious wild pain – a searching for something beyond
what the world contains"*

Bertrand Russell

lifetime gathering memories, only to lose them. If memory is the key to our identity then to lose our memory is to lose our very selves. Defining our identity in terms of memories is as inadequate as defining it in terms of our chemical make-up. So what about relationships? Can they help in our quest for identity?

A Passage to India

You know what it's like: you've just been introduced to someone at a party, and before you've had a chance to introduce yourself they drop into the would-be conversation the names of three celebrities they know. This appears to show how well connected they are, but actually demonstrates insecurity. Not confident enough that you will take them seriously for who they are, they attempt to gain significance by association.

To a certain extent, all of us are affected by this. We get a sinking feeling when the postman misses our house out. We collect autographs. We judge our popularity on the number of birthday cards we get. We put a counter on our blogs and websites. We want to be noticed and remembered by other people. Our identity as human beings has a relational element. Some of us find our value through our brothers, girlfriends, spouses or children. On the other hand, many of us feel valueless because we are unmarried or childless. There is certainly a great social pressure to be sociable. We are expected to be in a relationship, to be "in love", to have children, and to have good friends. Without these relationships we can often feel like nobodies.

We crave relationships. Yet we also live in a society in which many people are more aware of the daily affairs of celebrities or soap-opera characters than they are of their next-door neighbours. We think we know our neighbours, but often we have just an image of them based on their brand of car, the shopping bags going up the front path and the clothes on their visitors' backs. All these images of success are constantly programmed into us by the media. Even what we find attractive in the opposite sex seems to be influenced by others. In the Renaissance, voluptuousness was the pinnacle of beauty for women. But in the West today hard bodies and flat stomachs are the order of the day. Our tastes, goals and ambitions, and even our very understanding of who we are, are influenced by other people.

Although many of us believe our identity can be defined in terms of relationships, some of us also believe that our identity can be discovered independently. In the 1960s many people, in an effort to discover their true identity, "lost" themselves in India in order to find themselves. The backpacking urge continues on to our day unabated. However, we can never escape the influence of other people. Listen to where backpackers go, whom they meet and what they did. Their stories are fashionably similar. Backpackers are just influenced by a different set of people. As one writer has put it: "Wherever you go, there you are."[4]

A Brave New World

We cannot define ourselves simply in terms of sociological identity – as the result of the interactions we have with those around us. Nor can we define ourselves merely in terms of a psychological identity, based on what we remember about ourselves, or as a physical identity, based on our chemical composition. We need to be able to locate our identity in something more. Ironically, it is the great atheist philosopher Bertrand Russell who provides a clue to an alternative basis for identity:

"If I find in myself a desire which no experience in this world can satisfy, the most probable explanation is that I was made for another world."

C.S. Lewis

The centre of me is always and eternally a terrible pain - a curious wild pain - a searching for something beyond what the world contains. [5]

Bertrand Russell admitted here, at the end of his life, that right at the centre of his identity there was a hole. He felt a longing and a hunger for something more than he could find in the world. Human experiences and philosophies could not provide the satisfaction that he longed for, no matter what he tried. C.S. Lewis, an Oxford don and a renowned Christian thinker, made a famous suggestion which seems to answer Russell's longing with a very simple deduction:

If I find in myself a desire which no experience in this world can satisfy, the most probable explanation is that I was made for another world. [6]

Christians believe we were made as part of a plan for this world, but also that we were made for another world. Memory and relationships are important, but by themselves they are insufficient to define us. Similarly, our jobs and possessions are important, as are our careers and our aspirations, our bodies and our choices. We will find out more about this throughout the book. If we cannot be defined as an accident of nature, a collection of chemicals, a network of fragile relationships or an archive of fading memories, what is the alternative view of human identity that the Bible offers?

It's a Wonderful Life

A friend of mine was told she was an accident, and that her mother wished that she had had her aborted. That one piece of information led her to attempt suicide at sixteen. Many people believe that life is a cosmic accident and humanity is a freak of nature, a biological anomaly. However, even philosophers such as Bertrand Russell who want to conclude that life has no purpose find it very difficult to live consistently with this view. They still try to make the world a better place, care for the environment, and help their friends and neighbours. None of these activities makes any sense if life is, as someone has said, "like a blunt pencil, pointless".

Compare this with the description given to the origin of humanity in the Bible's opening chapter:

> **Then God said, 'Let us make human beings in our image, in our likeness, so that they may rule over the fish in the sea and the birds in the sky, over the livestock, and all the wild animals, and over the creatures that move along the ground'. (Genesis 1:26, TNIV)**

This extract from the Bible is mental dynamite and presents a completely different perspective on identity. Allow yourself to imagine temporarily that it could possibly be true. We will explore the difference that seeing life from this perspective could make to the way we see ourselves.

Just before this statement, there is a brief description of the origins of the universe. Christians through the centuries have seen this account as a wonderful display of God's power. He uses a few words to form billions of galaxies - it seems to be no big deal for every nebula, quasar, black hole and solar system to have been created from nothing. God creates the earth, and fills it with mountains and valleys, rivers and oceans, birds and fish and animal species beyond number. And then he comes to that which he was planning it all for. Human beings are the last things to be made - the finishing touch, the pinnacle.

I remember when we were expecting our first baby in our first home. The nesting instinct kicked in and we scrubbed and cleaned, wallpapered and decorated. We managed to fit more IKEA furniture into an ancient Volkswagen Golf than would seem humanly or legally possible. The AA was not impressed when we broke down because part of a flat-packed wardrobe had mashed the electrics of our car! We wanted to prepare the best environment for our new arrival. The last thing we brought into the room was our baby.

The creation account seems to mirror this experience. God prepared planet earth to receive humanity. If this is true, then human life is not just a cosmic accident but the deliberate act of a loving father. If we were born by design not chance, we have a purpose and an identity. Someone made us, someone wanted us to be here, and we are not an accident.

Picture Perfect

Immaculately dressed supermodels were walking along a beach sipping drinks. Then the screen cut to a simple message: "Image is nothing. Taste is everything. Drink Sprite." Sprite was the drink for people who wanted to convey the image that they didn't care about image! Image affects us at so many different levels. It is difficult for us to see who we really are behind the media projections. Our consumer choices define our image, but behind that is the quest for the right image, which as we have seen often drives our consumer choices. Perhaps our obsession with image derives from the fact that this is central to the design of humanity. We have seen that God made us and that we were not an accident. We also see that God made us to carry his image.

This is not saying that we physically resemble God or that God physically resembles us. Despite the language of the Bible that talks about the "eyes of the

Lord" or the "arm of the Lord", God is spirit, and he is everywhere. God does not have a physical body. He is not limited in space. So how do we carry God's image? The French theologian Henri Blocher describes the practice of Middle Eastern kings at about the time that Genesis was written.[7] They would set up images of themselves in the capital cities of conquered territories as physical reminders of their reign in their absence. Blocher argues that something similar is happening here. When human beings are given the title "image of God" our identity is defined as being representatives of God's rule over all creation. This is reinforced by God's mandate in the verse above: we are made to rule over the living world.

Thanks to my digital camera I take a lot more pictures than I keep. This is just as well. I often get the settings wrong. I sometimes leave the lens cap on. Some pictures are just bad. I took a nice one of the family out for a walk but inadvertently captured Granny's dog relieving herself. I seem to take a lot of portrait shots of my wife with her eyes closed. These images are disposable. We have seen that Christianity argues that we are not just chemicals, but that we have been designed by God to reflect his image and represent him. But, as bearers of God's image, are we disposable, or valuable?

There are three things that make an image valuable: who made the image, what the image depicts and the price someone will pay for that image.

Who made the image

Even my best artistic endeavours would not fetch a fraction of the price of a rough sketch by Leonardo da Vinci. To know that we were fearfully and wonderfully made by God, the creator of the world, gives us intrinsic value and identity. Our value in life is not dependent on what we have made of it, but on the fact that God made us.

What the image depicts

A paparazzi photographer can earn a fortune by catching the right person at the right time. The Christian world view argues that we are made in the image of the most significant and valuable being in the universe and this makes human life worth a fortune. We are often embarrassed by our external appearance, as we measure our worth by our relative beauty. But our image, whatever we think of it, is intrinsically valuable because it reflects God himself.

What someone will pay for the image

At the end of the day a picture is really worth only what someone will pay for it. Paparazzi photos and Leonardo da Vinci portraits are almost guaranteed big bucks. My local café, on the other hand, doubles as a gallery for local artists, and features ridiculous price tags. In my opinion, my primary-school children have painted better pictures that have ended up in the recycling bin! Are these pictures really worth £250? The fact that they still hang in the café week in, week out would suggest otherwise.

If it is true that an image is worth only what someone is willing to pay for it, then what would anyone pay for us? Are we worth any more than the £8 it would cost to buy our core chemical components from a hardware shop? In Chapter 4 we will see that the Bible teaches that God paid the price of his own Son's life for us. If this is true, then we know we are valuable beyond price.

I am expecting that one day somebody will produce a Hollywood film about the life of Mother Teresa of Calcutta. What I am not expecting is that Hollywood will depict Mother Teresa as a drunk who slept around with many men, swore and lived a life of luxury. Such a film would be an obscenity and a disgrace. The portrayal would fall far short of the truth of Mother Teresa's singular and sacrificial devotion to the poor and sick. Many an actress might find portraying her life very challenging, and the fact that no actress could live up to her reputation might explain why this film has not yet been made.

If we are made in God's image to represent his character on earth, then this role is a greater challenge than portraying Mother Teresa in a motion picture. Our being made in the image of God means that, when they look at our lives, those around us should be able to discern the very character of God. But we constantly misrepresent God by our inappropriate thoughts and actions. Instead of displaying the true character of a perfect God we display an ugly caricature. We fall short of God's reputation and God's calling on our lives. We will look further at the implications of this in Chapters 3 and 5. But we will also see how basing our fundamental identity on the fact that we are created by God, deliberately and for relationship with him, leads to significance in this life (Chapter 2) and eternity in the next (Chapter 6).

Identity

When I am introduced to somebody new, I often find myself being defined as Joel's dad, June's son, or Miriam's husband. It is quite acceptable to be defined in terms of a relationship. But I am more than this. I am a person in my own right. But I am more than this again. I am God's representative. This is the highest definition of identity possible. This is the Christian answer to the question: Who am I really?

Each of us, regardless of ability, gender, race or class, is valuable because God made us. Each of us has intrinsic dignity because we were created to represent

God. Each of us is significant because God thinks we are precious enough for him to pay the highest price possible. Our identity is first and foremost defined by this relationship to God. However, this does not totally dismiss the other clues we have to our identity. In this chapter we have seen that we try to define ourselves socially or relationally, psychologically or personally, and materially or environmentally. All these definitions of identity are inadequate by themselves, but together with relationship with God they make sense. These four aspects of life are the clues we will explore during the rest of this book.

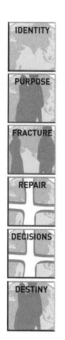

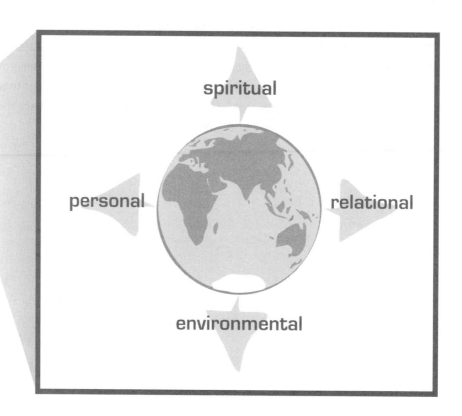

2

What am I supposed to be doing?

"Why do I do this everyday?" These words are scrawled in 6ft high grafitti on a long fence right by the side of the M40, a busy motorway feeding into London, The hundreds of thousands of drivers who pass those words are given the chance to step back and face a challenge. What am I doing spending my time in a traffic jam in the rain? Why am I always stuck behind an articulated lorry carrying "poisonous substances"? Why do I have to live so far away from my work? What is my job all about anyway? What is my life all about anyway? Surely I wasn't born to commute along the M40 day in, day out?

Personally, I suspect the train companies of maintaining the graffiti. It may just be a subtle advertising ploy to breed discontent with the popular commute by car in a futile attempt to revamp public transport's poor image.

Despite my cynicism, there is unfortunately a common resonance with the words on the fence. As we unload the dishwasher, walk the dog, brush our teeth, argue with our children or arrive late for work, we sympathize with the writer - why do we do this every day?

Perhaps it is a question we don't ask ourselves as often as we direct it at others. Why do you flick channels all the time? Why do you always leave your dirty washing on the floor? Why do you spend so long on the phone every day? Why do you always moan about your work? And then of course the people we live with find plenty of ammunition to fire back at us.

Whether via friend, family member or fence, we all face the question: "What are we supposed to be doing?" in one form or another. We all feel a need for a purpose that goes beyond the mundane, everyday features of our lives.

Twenty-five pairs of socks. That was what my mum sent me away with when I went to university. It was a stroke of genius. It meant I only needed one trip to the launderette a term. Once during my termly trip to wash my clothes the question hit me. As I was being slowly hypnotized by fifty socks in a tumble dryer, I saw my life in there too. Born, grow up, study, get a job, start a family, watch my kid being born, grow up, study ... and around and around it goes *ad infinitum*. Is life just an eternal spin cycle?

Clocks are circular, and so many of us believe time is too. The Danish philosopher Kierkegaard said that we should view life as more like an egg timer. As we watch the precious sands of time slipping away, irretrievably gone for good, he says: "For you everything is lost, eternity does not acknowledge you, it never knew you." This view of life is bleak. We are anonymous, momentary blips in the great scheme of things. We are stuck in a giant egg timer fighting against the swirling sands that one day will drag us down into oblivion.

I don't know which view of life is more depressing! Time going round and round for ever in a pointless cycle, or precious time slipping through our fingers? As I catch a few more grey hairs appearing on my head, and notice the lines developing around my eyes, it feels that Kierkegaard was closer to the mark. We don't want to waste our lives. We want answers. Our time is short, so what are we supposed to be doing with it?

Lost in Space

Waiting for Godot is an infuriating play to watch, because basically nothing happens. Two men wait for someone to turn up and in the end (forgive the spoiler) he doesn't! In the meantime, the two central characters reflect on the meaninglessness of life. This is what the playwright Samuel Beckett intends his audience to experience in the small-scale frustration of a play that goes nowhere. Some of us know exactly what he's getting at after enduring a staff meeting. Sometimes they are so dull that we feel as if the will to live is being sucked out of us! Some of us have felt like this waiting an hour for a bus that never arrived. Beckett writes about life:

> *They give birth astride of a grave, the light gleams an instant, then it's night once more.*

This desperate image demonstrates utter pessimism. The image is echoed in a recent Microsoft™ commercial that was so disturbing it was eventually banned from television in the UK. It shows a woman screaming as she gives birth to a baby boy, who flies out of her womb and out of the window. As the child flies through the air on its back, it screams and ages rapidly into an old man, eventually crashing at high speed into a grave. The screen turns black and then come the words: "Life is short. Play more. X Box". People were unsurprisingly offended by the uncensored quick succession of the traumas of birth, life and death. Yet the advert and Samuel Beckett were embracing a philosophy of life that is pretty common: eat, drink and be merry, for tomorrow we die.

"I went to the woods because I wished to live deliberately, to front only the essential facts of life, and see if I could not learn what it had to teach, and not, when I came to die, discover that I had not lived..."

Henry David Thoreau

Hero

Yet in a world in which we feel we are getting nowhere, where our efforts go by unappreciated, where nobody seems to care what happens to us, there is still a drive to push on. This spark of life can confront us in the most surprising of places: when we hear the introductory chords to a familiar song; when we breathe in the fresh morning air; or when we see a baby smile. I feel this spark watching epic movies. I know they are formulaic money-spinners, but I cannot stop myself enjoying them. When Russell Crowe plays Maximus in Gladiator, standing up to the corruption and cowardice of the Roman Empire, or when Mel Gibson plays William Wallace in Braveheart and takes on the might of the English establishment, I sense a hint of a purpose to life. These strong leaders know exactly who they are and why they are there. They are willing to sacrifice even their own lives for a noble cause. They are men on a mission, people of destiny. Someone once said that unless we have something we are willing to die for, we probably don't have anything worth living for either. This spark of life and sense of purpose is attractive. We want the same level of conviction that Maximus and Wallace had when we wonder what we are supposed to do with our lives.

It is the first day of term, and the new intake at Welton Academy nervously awaits their first lesson with the new English tutor, Mr Keating. For his first lesson he takes the boys out of the classroom and down to the trophy room. There he invites them to inspect the cases littered with medals, cups and awards. On the wall hang a myriad of team pictures all with young men, eyes ablaze, staring confidently and victoriously out into the room. That is when they hear the whisper, like a voice from the grave. They are told to seize the day and make their lives extraordinary. Carpe Diem. [8]

The film Dead Poets Society affected a lot of people of my generation. Many of my friends became teachers, inspired by the performance of Robin Williams. But not only were viewers struck by the potential impact they could have on young lives; many of my peers were also struck by the challenge of the film: What will you make of your life? A famous quotation from the film was taken from Henry David Thoreau's work Walden. This was one man's meditation in a secluded wood far away from the technological modernization that he feared was crippling his thought life. Thoreau wrote:

> *I went to the woods because I wished to live deliberately, to front only the essential facts of life, and see if I could not learn what it had to teach, and not, when I came to die, discover that I had not lived...* [9]

Many people feared getting to the end of their lives and finding out that they had never really lived. And so a generation grew up believing in Carpe Diem - seizing the day. In the late 1980s when the film was released, this motto began appearing on the ties of young City traders in London. It was obvious what life was about for them. It was about earning as much money as possible, as quickly as possible.

Vince Foster was one of the world's most influential lawyers and also Deputy Counsel to the President of the United States. Foster was asked to give a keynote speech at the School of Law at the University of Arkansas to students pursuing the "carpe diem" work ethic. During this speech he said: "You have amply demonstrated that you are achievers willing to work hard, long hours and set aside your personal lives, but it reminds me of that observation that no one was ever heard to say on his or her deathbed, 'I wish I had spent more time at the office.'"[10] Vince Foster was trying to persuade this room full of productive potential to see the relative insignificance of their work compared to the irreplaceable value of the people in their lives.

As we face the frustration of the daily commute or meaningless meetings at work; as we are inspired by feature films with heroic characters dying for what they believe in; as we face the challenge of Foster's bid to check our unbalanced lives with forward-looking hindsight, we are hit with a question. What are we supposed to be doing? It is often only at the end of our lives, as Foster pointed out, that we realize how much of it we have wasted on insignificant worries or activities. If we have only one shot at life, we need to get it right before we get to our deathbed full of regrets. What are we supposed to do with this precious gift of life? How do we make sure we use it well?

In the Line of Fire

I once found a plastic toy mobile phone outside my house. I asked passers-by if it belonged to them, but when it was not claimed I duly passed it on to my nine-month-old son. He used to hold it and chew it in the car, providing me with the peace of mind to concentrate on safe driving. A few months went by. On one occasion, while wiping off the saliva, I realized that the plastic "antenna" on the top was actually a button. Intrigued, I pressed it, expecting a sound effect. Instead, in front of my eyes shot a two-inch flame! It was no child's toy at all. It was a cigarette lighter in disguise. Literally flashing in front of my eyes, I imagined the danger I had put my son into every time we had gone anywhere in the car. He could have been burned, his clothes could have caught fire, he could have swallowed a mouthful of lighter fluid... He could have died.

Life is precious. We each have in our hands the gift of life, and we need to know what we should do with it. Are we supposed to play with it? What happens if we get to the end of our life and there is a button we are supposed to have pressed that shows us exactly what we should have done with it? What dangers could we be in if we misunderstand or misuse this gift? What are we supposed to be doing?

The very word "supposed" betrays an underlying assumption. It reveals that we think there is, should or could be a purpose, a plan and a path: a right way of living that will fulfil all the potential within us. A recent headline in The Times posed the question: "What is the meaning of life? Find out in Section 2". Inside they had the musings of contestants from a reality-TV show who had come to the conclusion that life was all about love. Section 2 also contained a single column from the evolutionary biologist Richard Dawkins, with his summary of the purpose of life. He concluded: "Living things are machines, programmed to preserve and propagate the genes that ride inside them ... that is the meaning of life in the scientific sense." His single column did not explain the justification of his invention of a self-generating machine. It did not excuse the devaluation of the human population to robots. It did not specify Mother Teresa as a failure of propagation. In fact, the reality-TV contestants did a better job of justifying their answer to the meaning of life! But both believed that there was something we are supposed to be doing.

When our conscience tells us we should be sponsoring our workmate as she runs to raise money for charity, or when we feel that we should be helping the elderly gentleman who has collapsed by the side of the road, or we should be looking after our bodies, or we should be fulfilling some potential or other, these feelings betray the fact that we believe there is meaning and purpose in the universe. They challenge us to reconsider the idea that life is a cosmic accident. Even my children know that these two views are mutually exclusive. They tell me far too often - "I didn't do it on purpose - it was an accident." As we saw in the last chapter, if there

"Man tries unsuccessfully to fill this void with everything that surrounds him, seeking in absent things the help he cannot find in those that are present, but all are incapable of it. This infinite abyss can be filled only with an infinite.. that is to say, God himself...   From the time we have forsaken him, it is a curious thing that nothing in nature has been capable of taking his place."

Blaise Pascal

is a God, then there is a design behind the universe, a reason that we exist, and something we are supposed to be doing.

Returning to the opening chapters of the Bible, we find not only answers to the mystery surrounding our identity, but also a clear mandate for life:

> *The LORD God took the man and put him in the Garden of Eden to work it and take care of it. And the LORD God commanded the man, "You are free to eat from any tree in the garden; but you must not eat from the tree of the knowledge of good and evil, for when you eat of it you will surely die." (Genesis 2:15-17)*

The Bible teaches that we are definitely not accidents. God takes the initiative to create human life, and right from the beginning provides a place and a purpose. We are made to live in the world and care for all that it contains. The job description given to us by God helps to define our reason for being. First of all, we were made to serve God, working under his direction and accountable to him. Our purpose has a spiritual dimension. Secondly, our purpose is beyond our own interests and involves looking out for others. It has a relational dimension. Thirdly, the purpose involves our interaction with the planet. It has an environmental dimension. Fourthly, this purpose has a personal dimension. Each of us has equal responsibility for the ongoing task. We cannot palm the responsibility off onto our neighbours, or our world leaders. We cannot do our bit and then tick it off on our to-do list.

To summarize, the purpose of human life cannot simply be defined in terms of love or procreation, as The Times suggested. According to the Bible, the meaning of life is a rich and complex combination of four key aspects: spiritual, relational, environmental and personal. These are the same four clues that we used to discover our identity in the last chapter. Let's take a closer look at these four aspects to see how they can answer the question: What are we supposed to be doing?

SPIRITUAL

C.S. Lewis wrote: "A baby feels hunger: well there is such a thing as food. A duckling wants to swim: well there is such a thing as water. Men feel sexual desire: well there is such a thing as sex." [11] Lewis goes on to argue that, just as physical appetites point to real physical things that fulfil them, so the universal hunger for the supernatural points to the existence of the divine. He explains that our instinct for purpose or meaning is strong evidence that God exists. When we travel around the world to cultures far and wide, we find an almost universal desire to worship because there really is a God to satisfy this longing. It looks like there is an inbuilt homing device in each one of us that draws beyond the mundane.

In the first chapters of the Bible, we see an intrinsic relationship between the creator and the created. This relationship involves communication and dependence for life. We see God involved in human beings' physical bodies and in their sleeping and eating, working and socializing. In other words, we see a spiritual dimension that encompasses all of life. In this initial picture of life there is no temple or church building and no official sacred space. Human beings were originally made to relate to God wherever they were and whatever they were doing.

The horror-movie industry likes to contradict this with spaces that are deemed more holy than others. There are church buildings that are hallowed ground where demons and evil spirits are not able to enter. This provides a safe zone for our noble heroes and heroines to dive into that is off limits to all manner of nefarious spiritual villains from the underworld. This reinforces a view of the world whereby God is safely contained in sacred times of the day in spiritual buildings.

In our increasingly compartmentalized lives, we need reminding that God intended our relationship with him to be integrated into the whole of life. The Bible teaches the amazing and liberating news that God is with us as we travel to work, to the hospital, to the church building and even to the ends of the earth. There is no separation between the sacred and the secular. There is no separation between spiritual life and everyday life. What the Bible begins to teach here in Genesis it reinforces throughout the rest of the book. What we should be doing with our life is enjoying the spiritual dimension of relationship with God.

RELATIONAL

The idea of "spirituality" often evokes an image of a Tibetan monk who has taken a vow of silence and lives in isolation in a remote monastery in the Himalayas. We have seen that we do not need to restrict our spiritual relationship with God to so-called "holy" places. Equally liberating is the fact that spirituality is not a private matter between us and God. Set against the backdrop of God's perfect creation in pristine condition, Genesis goes on to tell us that we were created for community:

> *The LORD God said, "It is not good for the man to be alone. I will make a helper suitable for him." Now the LORD God had formed out of the ground all the beasts of the field and all the birds of the air. He brought them to the man to see what he would name them; and whatever the man called each living creature, that was its name. So the man gave names to all the livestock, the birds of the air and all the beasts of the field. (Genesis 2:18-20)*

The first chapter of Genesis contains a repetitive chorus: "And God saw that it was good." But as we read the account of this good and perfect world, we stumble over the words: "It is not good." The only thing that was not good in this perfect world was isolation. We have seen that we were intended for a relationship with God but, even when this was perfectly in place, it was insufficient.

God did not need human beings to fulfil him, as he was already perfectly fulfilled. But the single living human was not yet fulfilled. One human by himself could not fully reflect the image of God. When God said: "Let us make man in our own image," there was a surprising plural! To whom are "us" and "our" referring?

It is important to introduce a central but complicated element of the Christian faith at this point. Christians refer to God as the Trinity, by which they mean God the Father, Son and Holy Spirit. This is not a belief in three gods. It is the belief that the one being of God is three persons in relationship. Christians find this very complicated and use illustrations to try to make it clearer. St Patrick, the patron saint of Ireland, famously likened God to a shamrock, a stem of clover with three leaves. Others have used the illustration of a man who is simultaneously a father, a son and a husband. These illustrations, while initially helpful, are ultimately inadequate because they don't describe the reality of God as a united community.

The concept of Trinity may be beyond our understanding, but what it does show is God in relationship. Being made in his image shows us that relationships are an important clue to life. There have been many millions of songs, films and books written about love, concluding that love is the key to life. This finds resonance both with our natural understanding of the meaning of life (going back to the musings in The Times) and also with the Christian faith.

The poet John Donne famously wrote:

> *No man is an island, entire of itself; every man is a piece of the continent, a part of the main.*

This rings true to our experience. We crave relationships and we need family and friends. One of the harshest forms of torture is solitary confinement. One of the most painful forms of emotional abuse is neglect. Without the opportunity to interact with other people, all of us struggle to maintain our sanity and our humanity.

Nick Hornby, in his excellent novel About a Boy, provides a cameo of the adult adolescent male in the West today. Will, the ultimate cad, challenges Donne's poem with his own philosophy of "I am an island; I am Ibiza." Will is oblivious to others around him, living for his own pleasure in splendid isolation. As the story unfolds Hornby shows that, despite his best efforts, Will's life will prove shallow and empty if he doesn't take responsibility for those around him. It doesn't take a rocket scientist to guess that the book is about Will's transformation from a 38-year-old boy to a 38-year-old man, from an island man to a family man.

When asked by the religious leaders in his day which of the commandments were more important, Jesus answered in a way that shocked them all and yet succinctly summarized thousands of words of divine revelation:

> *Love the Lord your God with all your heart and with all your soul and with all your strength and with all your mind; and, Love your neighbour as yourself. (Luke 10:27)*

God's purpose for life is that we love him in every aspect of our lives but also that we share that love with every human being. Why does it feel comfortable when we give up our seat for an elderly person on the bus? Why do we feel satisfaction in giving aid to the starving in the two-thirds world? Why do we feel at home when we buy The Big Issue from a homeless person?

Most of us hope that if we are nice to people, then people will be nice to us. But this view by itself makes every act of kindness actually an act of selfishness, and robs us of the possibility of doing any genuinely selfless and kind action. Christianity presents another possibility. We enjoy being generous and compassionate. Not because of an accidental wiring of our brains, or because of some psychological need to feel good about ourselves. But because we are connecting with our central purpose in life, to demonstrate God's love in our world.

ENVIRONMENTAL

But for Adam no suitable helper was found. So the LORD God caused the man to fall into a deep sleep; and while he was sleeping, he took one of the man's ribs and closed up the place with flesh. Then the LORD God made a woman from the rib he had taken out of the man, and he brought her to the man.

The man said,

"This is now bone of my bones
and flesh of my flesh;
she shall be called 'woman',
for she was taken out of man."
For this reason a man will leave his father and mother and be united to his wife, and they will become one flesh. (Genesis 2:20-24)

Adam's job was to name and care for the living things on the planet. But this was not to be done in isolation. He was also created to love and to be loved. He was made in God's image of community. He needed a helper and so God created Eve. This helper position should not be understood in terms of a slave role or even as an employee, but rather as a colleague, equally responsible for the task in hand.

Responsibility for the world around us is innate to each one of us. Whenever we marvel at a beautiful sunset, when we take pleasure in tending our garden or when we feel outrage as seabirds and sea mammals are affected by an oil spillage, we sense connection with the world around us. This connection between ourselves and the natural world is simple - we share a creator.

God created work for us, not a necessary evil to pay the bills, but as part of our purpose in life. Work is a privilege. It gives us significance and it helps us be like God. In fact, we should all have the job title "caretaker" first and foremost above our other titles. This is our specified job in the world.

Our paid work is not just a secondary affair, however. Whatever job we do, we can somehow be connected by it to God and the world around us. If we are nurses, teachers, policemen, accountants, lawyers, supermarket checkout assistants or builders, if we buy fairly traded coffee or support a charitable cause, then we are taking care of the needs of the people God created. If we are vets or town planners or allotment owners, if we take care of a pet, water the office plants, recycle, conserve energy, take public transport or give up smoking, then we are protecting the environment God made. If we are artists or architects, designers or decorators, then we reflect God's creative nature. If we are caretakers, administrators, cleaners or repair technicians, then we reflect God's sustaining nature. This perspective is vital to the question: What am I supposed to do with my

"every man has forgotten who he is. One may understand the cosmos, but never the ego: the self is more distant than any star."

G.K. Chesterton

life? The Christian world view gives meaning, significance and dignity to our daily work. It gives us an answer to the question: Why do I do this every day?

PERSONAL

I was invited to a party, and so I carefully picked out my best shirt and jeans, went round to my friend's house and knocked on the door. When I went in I bumped into a guy wearing a ridiculous outfit - with flared trousers and big hair. I felt embarrassed for him because he looked so silly. But as I looked round, I saw that everybody was wearing the loudest, most outrageous '70s costumes. I was surrounded by frill-front shirts, kipper ties and gold medallions. And then I felt embarrassed for me. I was the one who looked silly, not any of these friends in their loud, outdated, unfashionable fancy dress. I was the odd one out.

Shame is a dreadful thing. It makes us sitting targets for the media, as we are desperate to fit in. The advertising industry takes full advantage of this and offers us targets that we are unable to meet. We can never look like Barbie or the pop stars and cat walk models. Yet still we spend copious amounts of money and buy countless products that claim to give us that look. Still we feel the need to shed a few pounds, impress the right people, dress the right way. We still feel easily embarrassed.

At the end of the account of the creation of Adam and Eve, there is a final and important observation:

The man and his wife were both naked, and they felt no shame. (Genesis 2:25)

God made us in his image and in a perfect world there should have been no shame, either before God or before other people. We know we should not worry about how we look or how we are perceived. Yet these concerns often drive us in life and affect everything that we do.

Our society teaches us that we should be ashamed of how we look. This shame affects what we wear and, in turn, how we relate to one another. The Bible reverses this order. Adam and Eve related to one another as God intended. This affected how they dressed, and the result was no shame. When we relate to one another as God intends, we need not worry about how we look or whether we are wearing fashionable clothes. Shame is gone.

Proof of Life

The old story goes that it was a foggy night and two Navy sailors on a pub crawl were lost on their way to the next bar, slightly the worse for wear. Just then the admiral of the fleet walked down the street, but all the inebriated sailors saw was a chance to ask for some help: "Oy, mate! D'you knows where we are?" To which the irate admiral replied: "Do you know who I am?" The sailors put a comforting arm round the admiral and said: "Mate, we thought we was in a bad way, but you must be in real trouble if you don't even knows who you are."[12]

We have seen that the nagging questions we face about who we really are can find some resolution in the idea that human beings are made in God's image. But why did he bother in the first place? Is life just a terminal sexually transmitted disease? Is it just a short journey between two hospitals? What is life all about and what are we supposed to be doing with it?

God related to the first human he created in a perfect two-way relationship. When he looked in the mirror at himself, he felt no shame, and when he related to others around him, they were equals and they got along. Together they were caretakers of the world that God had made.

This is a picture of peace. The diagram we introduced in the last chapter shows that man is now at peace with God, with other people, with the world around him and with himself. The diagram shows us what our purpose is in life. When we wonder what we are supposed to be doing with our life, what we are really doing is craving this peace. It is not a passive peace but a dynamic peace. It is not the sort of peace we get on our days off. It is a peace we work for. This peace allows us to find harmony in our environment, integrity in our personal lives, support in our relationships, and intimacy with God.

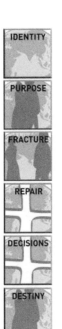

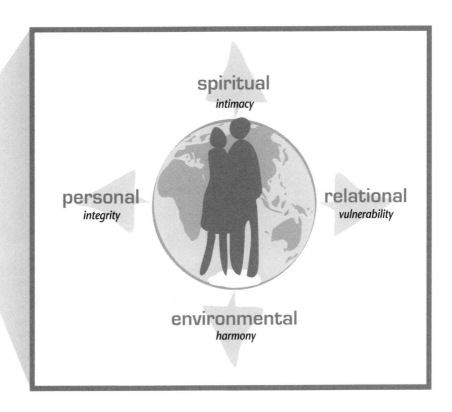

3

Why am I so mixed up?

A hideous monster stalks the streets of London. Meanwhile, a young man from a privileged background studies hard and becomes a doctor. A bright future seems laid out before him, but he has been struggling with a dark side to his character that he can't understand. Unable to reconcile what he does with who he wants to be, he has embarked on a daring experiment to try to separate out the two natures he finds within himself. He concocts an elixir that transforms him into the monstrous night-time stalker. This alter ego seems to be evil incarnate. This is of course the premise to Robert Louis Stephenson's classic novel Dr Jekyll and Mr Hyde, which explores the opposing characters that we all find within ourselves.

This theme has also captured the imagination of science-fiction writers. Captain Kirk of Star Trek fame was once involved in a bizarre transporter malfunction that left him briefly separated into two people that existed simultaneously; one good, one evil. Spiderman 3 features an internal struggle between the light and dark natures of Peter Parker, mirroring the same battle Superman faced in Superman 2. David Fincher's fine film Fight Club wrestles with the internal struggle between good and evil that is taking place in a man with a dreary life and a dreary job.

What Stephenson recognized as human nature is echoed by the Russian dissident Alexander Solzhenitsyn in his powerful account of the brutality of Stalin's atrocities, based on his own experience of eight years in a Soviet prison. After being on the receiving end of persecution and suffering, you would expect anyone to dismiss the regime as evil. Solzhenitsyn, however, offers a far more perceptive analysis:

> *If only it were all so simple! If only there were evil people somewhere insidiously committing evil deeds, and it were necessary only to separate them from the rest of us and destroy them. But the line dividing good and evil cuts through the heart of every human being. And who is willing to destroy a piece of his own heart?[13]*

Solzhenitsyn describes a problem we all face: an inner battle between good and evil. We know what we ought to do, but will we do it? I feel this battle every time I pass a kebab shop. One side tells me to give in to temptation - it won't hurt. The other side reminds me to think about my body mass index! I see my children noticing the battle in me, when I have been short-tempered with them for no reason, only to be polite and pleasant when the phone rings seconds later. I can go out of my way to allow one car into the flow of traffic, and then selfishly steal a parking space ahead of somebody who has been waiting. How did this mixture of good and evil, beauty and ugliness, pain and pleasure end up inside us? Why am I so mixed up?

Fight Club

We often like to think of ourselves as basically good people. So long as we are not hurting anyone and we are no worse than the average person, we congratulate ourselves that we are doing OK. And if we put money in the charity box and do our neighbours an occasional favour, then we feel the scales are tipping on the right side of the balance.

"the line dividing good and evil cuts through the heart of every human being"

Alexander Solzhenitsin

Some of us are so caught up in our own gifts, abilities and good works that we don't see our failings. But other household members could probably fill a large notebook with them. Others of us self-evaluate far too critically and are weighed down by guilt and shame. However hard we try, we still lose our tempers, focus on our mistakes and feel lousy about ourselves. We hardly notice when our closest friends encourage us with compliments.

When we take the time to reflect properly on who we are, we see compassion, patience, courage and self-restraint living alongside occasions of being vindictive, selfish, lustful and bad-tempered. Which set of attitudes are our true colours? Dr Jekyll and Mr Hyde suggest that we need to face up to the fact that we are a mixture of both good and evil.

This mixture is not just present at a personal level. We can see it on a global scale. The ingenuity and technical brilliance humankind demonstrated in putting a man on the moon is also responsible for the horrors of the gas chambers of the Holocaust. We can use our mobile phones to aid fair trade in the third world, but also to circulate videos of torture. We can rely on our local Chinese restaurant for our takeaways, but still be capable of marginalizing ethnic minorities in the workplace.

This mixture of nobility and savagery is present in the natural world too. The same wind that can blow clouds across the sky to provide the perfect frame for the setting sun can whip itself up into a hurricane that will make thousands homeless and rob hundreds of their lives. The lioness that protects and plays with her own young will chase, strangle and consume a baby zebra.

We need an explanation of the bittersweet symphony that is life. We need a way to account for the combination of benevolence and malevolence that we see in ourselves, in our race and in our world. Coming to terms with this will help us in our quest for our identity and purpose.

The Devil's Advocate

If you had visited me in my home on 5 September 2005, you would have got the impression that I was an unsociable and untidy person, who collected cardboard boxes for a hobby and was minimalist with regard to furnishings. I would not have offered you a coffee, nor would I have had time for a proper conversation. In fact, I would probably have either asked you to leave or handed you a mop! But if I had the chance, I would explain that this was not the way I usually lived. I was just moving in and was in the process of trying to make a lovely house a home.

An amusing recent advertisement made the point backwards. A girl, noticing that a boy in her block of flats had left his front door open, looked at the upheaval that was his lounge and called the police! When she told him the bad news that he had been burgled, he decided it was time to use the Yellow Pages and pay for a cleaner!

On a warm summer's evening in the countryside it is hard not to feel the intensity of the beauty of our world. Yet it takes only a few moments after switching on the television news for us to realize that we are also living in a broken and damaged world. How can the two extremes co-exist?

Looking around, you might think that God is neither powerful nor loving. If God really were powerful then he would do something about the suffering, and if he really were loving then he wouldn't just sit there and do nothing. But hearing the full story can help. A messy house could be explained by new occupants moving in, a burglary or bad management. We need to find out whether there is bigger story that can explain the state of our world, and the state of our own souls.

The first few chapters of the Bible narrate an incident that claims to explain why the world is in such a mess. Before we look at it, let's recap the world view that Genesis has already described.

God has created the world and appointed humanity to be his representatives and caretakers, enjoying intimacy with him, significance in work and meaningful relationships within a community. In this context we live in peace with ourselves, others, God and the world. We know exactly who we are and what we are supposed to be doing with our lives. With chapters 1 and 2 echoing in our ears as an idyllic and perfect world, Genesis chapter 3 is a total catastrophe. The place is turned upside down.

> *Now the serpent was more crafty than any of the wild animals the LORD God had made. He said to the woman, "Did God really say, 'You must not eat from any tree in the garden'?"*
>
> *The woman said to the serpent, "We may eat fruit from the trees in the garden, but God did say, 'You must not eat fruit from the tree that is in the middle of the garden, and you must not touch it, or you will die.'"*
>
> *"You will not surely die," the serpent said to the woman. "For God knows that when you eat of it your eyes will be opened, and you will be like God, knowing good and evil." (Genesis 3:1-4)*

Genesis 1 introduces us to God, the main character of the unfolding story, the creator and sustainer of the universe. The next characters we come across are Adam and Eve - our earliest ancestors. They enjoyed God's perfect creation and understood what it meant to live in peace - spiritually, socially, personally and environmentally. Now we are introduced to a fourth character - the serpent. We are not told where he came from, but his motivations are clear. He is hell-bent on destroying the perfect world God has set up. He uses a strategy that's still in evidence today. This strategy has persisted through the centuries and still trips us up on a regular basis.

Dissatisfy the customer

A salesman who wants to sell refrigerators to Eskimos needs to be as cunning as the serpent in this passage! Adam and Eve are living in the perfect environment. They have no need for anything. What could a serpent possibly have to offer them? His strategy is to breed dissatisfaction, even within paradise.

This is significant for life in a consumer culture. Marketing managers and advertising gurus rely on the fact that they are able to spread dissatisfaction and make us want things we never knew we needed. We may be richer and healthier than we have ever been before, but we are more dissatisfied than ever. Only 50 years ago, nobody knew what a computer was. Now nearly everyone has one, but the magazines are still trying to persuade us to buy the latest model. How on earth did people travel from A to B without a global positioning system? However did people have time to wash dishes? Whether it is disposable nappies, ring tones or individual savings accounts, the media has done a great job in breeding dissatisfaction. We are convinced that many things are essential for life that our grandparents were blissfully unaware of.

When the serpent got Adam and Eve to look at the fruit and lick their lips, he was well on his way to success. When an alcoholic pauses by the drinks aisle in the supermarket, the temptation suddenly becomes overwhelming. When we even notice advertisements for loans, fast cars or tax cheats, seeds of dissatisfaction have been sown.

Distort the command

The serpent's chat-up line manages to put a negative spin on all that God has provided. "Did God really say that you should not eat from any tree of the garden?" The serpent's first words to human beings encourage them to doubt God's words and his generosity. The serpent knew that he had to usurp God's primary place in Adam and Eve's life to tempt them away from God.

This is pervasive even today. Reading the Bible is almost a taboo in this century, especially if it is to find out what God has to say to us. We often approach it with cynicism and doubt. God's name, as well as his words, is regularly mocked in the media. Living without reference to God is easiest when it is trendy to doubt what God has said.

Deny the consequences

The serpent has set himself up for the lie - the direct contradiction "You will not surely die." He would not have been given the time of day if he had started out with this line, but he has already managed to breed doubt and dissatisfaction, and he now has a captive audience ready to believe anything. The butter-wouldn't-melt-in-his-mouth serpent even intimates that God is the liar.

This tactic of denying consequences can still be seen today. Packets of cigarettes may have warnings emblazoned on them: "Smoking Leads to Lung Cancer." But kebab vans don't tell you about the dangers of heart disease as they offer you extra mayonnaise, nor do travel agents warn you of the risks of exposure to the sun as you book your two-week, five-star, all-inclusive package deal in Tunisia. If advertisers are forced to warn you about the implications of spending beyond your means as you purchase a new three-piece suite on instant credit, they microscopically etch them in fine print on the back page using vocabulary that only a legal expert could decipher.

Deride the character of God

Finally, the serpent insinuates that God is nervous about any kind of rivalry between himself and humanity. He tells the couple that, if they were to eat the fruit, God would be unable to keep them weak. The serpent was guilty of inciting mutiny against the creator.

Alongside honest questions, there is often a temptation to question God's character. Does he exist? Does he really love us? Does he really want what is best for us? Does he really care about the wars raging around the world? Perhaps he will let us all off the hook at the end of the day. Perhaps he won't mind one little sin... If your friend falsely accuses you of stealing from him, you would be offended. When we challenge God's character, we offend him in the same way.

The serpent puts the cherry on the cake. He has caused Adam and Eve to discount God's words, and to listen to him instead. He has caused Adam and Eve to eat what they should not eat. Now to top it all he has persuaded them to view their provider as a liar and a coward.

This incident provides the source code for a virus that has infected every single thing on planet earth. Like a computer virus, it is invisible, aggressive and invasive, not necessarily immobilizing the computer immediately, but wreaking insidious havoc under the surface. This invisible havoc inside us and every living thing answers the question of why we feel so messed up and mixed up, and helps us understand why the answer to the question "What are we supposed to be doing?" seems both attractive and unattainable. Using the four relationships that originally described peace, we will see how this incident damaged everything.

SPIRITUAL

When the woman saw that the fruit of the tree was good for food and pleasing to the eye, and also desirable for gaining wisdom, she took some and ate it. She also gave some to her husband, who was with her, and he ate it. Then the eyes of both of them were opened, and they realized they were naked; so they sewed fig leaves together and made coverings for themselves. (Genesis 3:6-7)

We have some tough rules in our household! Don't put your fingers in the plug socket. Don't eat food that's been on the floor for more than ten seconds. Do chew before swallowing. Don't leave skateboards on the staircase. By instituting rules I, as a parent, am not trying to repress my children's freedom. I am expressing my love for them. When any child disobeys their parents it is painful because most of the rules parents establish are there to protect the child. When children break rules they are putting either their own or other people's immediate or long-term well-being in jeopardy. It is extra painful because they are also implying that they distrust our judgement or our love.

God feels the pain of betrayal and distrust as he watches Adam and Eve break the only rule that he set for them. This lack of trust and respect breaks the perfection of the relationship. This is partly because lack of trust makes any relationship virtually impossible. It is also because a morally pure God cannot stand even the slightest speck of evil. Breaking the command, and breaking the relationship, was wrong, and resulted in separation.

As soon as Adam and Eve hear God walking in the garden, they show that they are fully aware of their betrayal. They run and hide from him. God had given them the garden and all that was in it as a gift. It was supposed to be a space where they could demonstrate their allegiance to him. But they use it to build a barrier to shut him out. The sheer futility of trying to hide from God is pathetic. Their perfect relationship with God is damaged and there is spiritual separation and breakdown.

RELATIONAL

Then the man and his wife heard the sound of the LORD God as he was walking in the garden in the cool of the day, and they hid from the LORD God among the trees of the garden. But the LORD God called to the man, "Where are you?"

He answered, "I heard you in the garden, and I was afraid because I was naked; so I hid."
And he said, "Who told you that you were naked? Have you eaten from the tree that I commanded you not to eat from?"
The man said, "The woman you put here with me - she gave me some fruit from the tree, and I ate it."
Then the LORD God said to the woman, "What is this you have done?" The woman said, "The serpent deceived me, and I ate." (Genesis 3:8-13)

"*I see many people die because they judge that life is not worth living. I see others paradoxically getting killed for the ideas or illusions that give them a reason for living... I therefore conclude that the meaning of life is the most urgent of questions.*"

Albert Camus

As soon as human beings rebel against God there is an immediate social impact. Not only do they hide from God, but they realize they are naked and so hide themselves from each other. Nakedness is no longer appropriate because human beings cannot enjoy the transparency of relationship they once knew. Relationships are marked by a need for protection and distance from one another. Again, they use creation in a way in which it was never intended. They use it to build barriers. When human beings are disconnected from God they become simultaneously disconnected from each other. According to the Bible, it is at this point that bullying, war and racism entered our world. Later, God announces the battle of the sexes. But they had already begun to feel these consequences as they blamed each other for their own wrongdoing. The man has lost his helper and acquired a sparring partner. There is alienation.

We know we were made for relationships, and friends and family can bring us the deepest joy in our lives. Yet we also know that it is those same people that can hurt us the most deeply. In fact, the closer we are to someone, the more extreme the joy and also the pain they can cause us. Christianity helps us to understand this experience. We were originally designed for the joy of friendship, but when our relationship with God is out of kilter it has a knock-on effect. Breakdown and pain become part and parcel of all our relationships.

ENVIRONMENTAL

To Adam he said, "Because you listened to your wife and ate from the tree about which I commanded you, 'You must not eat of it,'

"Cursed is the ground because of you; through painful toil you will eat of it all the days of your life. It will produce thorns and thistles for you, and you will eat the plants of the field. By the sweat of your brow you will eat your food until you return to the ground, since from it you were taken; for dust you are and to dust you will return." (Genesis 3:17-19)

One small bite for Adam and Eve was a giant fall for humanity. When human beings listened to the serpent the world was turned upside down. The serpent was part of the creation that humanity was supposed to rule over under God's guidance. Our relationship with creation was totally confused when humanity decided not to rule over the snake, but to listen to him. He took God's place in our lives, and God was relegated as we deemed him subordinate. There are spiritual and relational knock-on effects, as we have seen; but the physical world we were supposed to take care of is also in utter confusion. The perfect creation is now in perfect chaos.

We cannot fully understand the interconnectedness of life on earth. Who would have thought that spraying deodorant on your armpits in the UK would have an effect on the likelihood of sunbathers in Australia developing skin cancer? Chaos theory argues that small changes in a system can have a massive effect: a butterfly flapping its wings in Europe could be the trigger for a series of events leading to a hurricane in the Bahamas. Hurricanes, earthquakes, tsunamis, plagues and famine were not the way God originally created the world. Just as a small piece of code in a computer virus can bring down a mighty business's network, so the insidious virus we call sin means that all our actions have knock-on effects.

In the aftermath of the betrayal, God curses the ground. Nature has now been affected by humanity's rebellion against God. Now drought, disaster and disease are as much apart of the natural world as dew, deer and daffodils. We live in an environment of beauty and brokenness. This affects the work we do in this world. When God cursed the ground he was making human work into a battle for survival. We experience this battle even in an air-conditioned office with leather seats and wireless networks. We get that Monday-morning feeling. We get tired, stressed and sick. We may understand that work gives us significance, but work is not always easy. In fact, work is often frustrating.

PERSONAL

The final result of the disobedience was that our inner peace was damaged. As well as a sense of frustration replacing the sense of significance we had from our responsibilities, we can no longer look in the mirror the same way. We looked in Chapter 1 at why we struggle so much with the concept of identity, and this chapter gives us the answer. We may be made in the image of God, but we have failed to live up to his image.

This failing introduced a new set of emotions. Firstly, there was shame. Secondly, there was fear. These made Adam and Eve instinctively want to run and hide. Thirdly, their consciences are engaged in a battle with them. They know they have done wrong, and yet they still try to blame anyone but themselves. They blame each other. They blame the serpent. They even dare to blame God for creating them in the first place. They know they should own up, but they don't. They know they should apologize, but they don't. Fourthly, there was meaninglessness to their existence because their lives would end with death. They had become aware of that eternal spin cycle in which we begin as dust, spend our years fighting the weeds and the thistles, and then return to dust. Being separated from God makes our lives meaningless.

We still live in shame before other people, in fear of God and in a battle with our own conscience. We still try to blame God and lay the responsibility for war, natural disasters and our own personality disorders at his door. We still feel confused, frustrated and anxious. We still try persistently to leave God out of the equation, although ultimately that sort of existence is pointless because all we were is dust, and that is all we will become. We have lost meaning and integrity in our lives.

The four relationships that were in perfect order at the beginning of time and are the key to understanding our identity, purpose and destiny have been turned upside down by the first sin. This world we live in now is damaged in all those relational dimensions, which explains the separation, alienation, frustration and disintegration that we see and feel. But none of the relationships were broken completely or irreparably. Even in this chapter, at history's darkest moment, there are glimmers of hope.

Although the crime has been committed and the damage has been done, Adam and Eve are still there. God does not destroy them immediately. He comes into the garden, draws them out of their hiding places and talks to them about what went wrong. God, justifiably angry, is gracious and compassionate and gentle. He maintains his love for humanity, despite needing to exact a just punishment for their behaviour.

Adam and Eve are punished and are banished from the garden. However, even outside paradise, the world was full of beauty and food and shelter. Although God did not walk physically with them as in the garden, his presence was still felt. Although their relationship with each other was strained, they were still companions on a journey. Although their relationship with the earth was still one of frustration, they were still able to work and manage the land to produce food. Their fundamental identity was fractured at every turn, but not completely lost. They would look in the mirror and feel ashamed, but they would also remember that they were made in the image of God.

Six Degrees of Separation

This brings us back to our original question. Why do we feel so mixed up? Our ideal world is fractured, but we still feel the pulls to peaceful relationship with God, others, self and the world. We still enjoy to some degree the spiritual, relational, environmental and personal aspects of life. But in our everyday experience we also struggle with separation, alienation, frustration and disintegration. We also struggle with the viral qualities of the underlying cause - the choice to turn away from God.

The Bible calls this ongoing tendency in each of us to rebel against God "sin". We live in a culture that struggles with the idea of sin. We have no problem in labelling certain things as evil - bombings, paedophiles, serial killers or genocide. However, we still tend to try to pass the buck of responsibility, even for these evil acts of injustice, just as Adam and Eve did. We blame parents, teachers, societies, cultures or propagandists. When we do wrong we excuse ourselves by saying we are only human. This sounds like we are implying a design flaw. Implicitly our excuses pass the blame back to God for not designing us correctly in the first place. We shy away from calling such things "sin".

Adam and Eve took a bite of fruit. That seemingly trivial action was actually incredibly significant, not just because it was breaking a command but because it was breaking a relationship. Our seemingly minor offences do not just break the laws of an invisible deity; they betray the trust of a heavenly Father. Deliberately continuing to do this is what the Bible means by sin.

C.S. Lewis tries to help us understand this through his character Edmund in The Chronicles of Narnia. The White Witch offers him Turkish delight. When he bites into that trivial treat, he enters into relationship with the White Witch. This puts him on the opposing side to Aslan, the good ruler of Narnia. Edmund also becomes addicted to it, wanting more and willing even to betray his own siblings for another bite.

The answer to the question of why we feel mixed up is that we are mixed up. We do have both Jekyll and Hyde inside us. Our noble elements reflect the way that we were originally made. Yet we are infected by the virus of sin. By returning to our diagram we can see that each of the relationships is still there, no longer in peace, but in breakdown.

Even small acts of betrayal of God - disregard, disrespect or disobedience - place us firmly on the side of sin. This is a bleak picture of the whole of humanity infected with an incurable disease that means struggle in every dimension of our lives. We feel the pain of separation, alienation, disintegration and frustration. But this is not the end of the story. In fact, it is only page three of several thousand pages of an unfolding drama of rescue. We will see in the next chapters what God expects us to do with this mess.

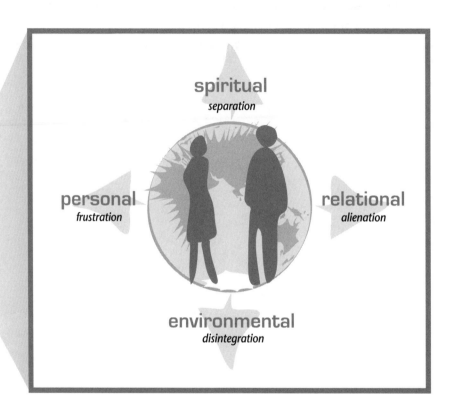

4

What on earth is going on?

I have no memory of my 22nd birthday. I count a

landmark birthday as one on which one reaches an age that (normally) ends in a nought or a five, although I have to admit that thirteen was also quite a big deal for me! These landmarks can force us to re-evaluate what life is about. When the number in the tens column changes we become more aware of the shortness of life.

Thirteen Going On Thirty

When I was thirteen I thought that being thirty meant being really old. I thought we would have invented cold fusion and we'd be whizzing around the planets in our personal space vehicles. When I turned thirty, I realized the world had not progressed half as much as I had expected. I also realized I had not achieved half of what I expected to. Then I began to notice that quite a lot was written on what I should have achieved in my life. I saw lists in books and magazines along the lines of "Fifty things you should do before you are thirty"! I was fascinated. I read them all through. And each time I kept thinking that it was too late! I had never climbed the Eiffel Tower, shot anything, or shaken hands with a Member of Parliament! I had never driven a sports car, run a marathon or missed a plane! I have still never fallen off a horse, returned a piece of furniture to IKEA or been dry-slope skiing! I have failed in all these significant life achievements. These lists made me feel as if my life was over and I had missed the point. I should have seen these books when I was twenty, so I could at least have had a chance of achieving them! Even better would be if a definitive list was published, and I had memorized it at preschool!

As I was coming to terms with my failure, I realized that many people around me really were living as though their destiny consisted of achieving an imaginary list of random goals, egged on by friends and media alike. They were giving and receiving red-letter days for their birthdays. They were jumping on aeroplanes and even jumping off aeroplanes! But I wonder whether they will manage the entire list of lists by the time they are thirty. What if they fail - like me? What then? What if the scenario is even worse; what if they get to thirty and find out that they have not even achieved the goals they set themselves?

In his collection of short stories entitled Life After God, the master of the zeitgeist novel Douglas Coupland writes about a man who is tracking down the friends he used to hang out with as a teenager. On the journey the main character pauses to reflect on his own life:

> *Some facts about me, I think I am a broken person. I seriously question the road my life has taken and I endlessly rehash the compromises I have made in my life. I have an insecure and vaguely crappy job with an amoral corporation so that I don't have to worry about money. I put up with halfway relationships so as not to worry about loneliness. I have lost the ability to recapture the purer feelings of my younger years in exchange for a streamlined narrow-mindedness that I assumed would propel me to the top. What a joke.*[14]

The honesty in this quotation is arresting. Many of us don't stop long enough to check where we have come to in our lives. If we do stop, the big question is: How on earth did we get here? Where we are now is not the place where we thought we would end up when we were younger. Who we are is not the person we thought we would be when we were younger. What a joke.

I would like to challenge the list of things I was supposed to have done by the time I was thirty How do the people that write these lists know what we should be doing? For all of us this is our first shot at life, even those who are on their next life stage. Even the kindly people who stop me in the street and advise me not to waste the precious time with my children are able to pass on their wisdom only from having been here once before. Is the list just a compilation of regrets? Is there anyone who could write a definitive list of important things to do with life? Who could possibly know?

Sometimes when my preschool children show me their artistic masterpieces, I smile admiringly, pore over the scribbles and tell them what a wonderful picture it is. I say that I have never seen such a fantastic drawing and that it deserves to hang in pride of place on the inside of the recycling bin... I mean, on the fridge door! Of course, I never ask them what it is. That would be terribly offensive. So I ask them to explain how they drew it. If they tell me that the long wiggly-line worm has eaten a large plate of spaghetti and then crawled back under the wild zigzag grass, I begin to see some method in the madness. Now I am genuinely impressed both with the imagination and with the penmanship! I appreciate the mess as a potential career in art and design!

We all need to have a bit more information before assigning our lives to the recycle bin. We need to have information from the designer. As we look around at the mess that is planet earth, we need to ask the creator what the purpose of it all is. It is only as we discover this purpose in the midst of the mess that we will know whether we are really aiming at the right goals in our lives.

The Hole

The road outside our house is always being dug up. The man from the water board digs an enormous trench for half a day, causing long queues of irate drivers. He takes his time doing his work and then spends a couple of hours filling it in and making the road surface good. Then before you know it the gas engineers are out digging another trench, blocking the traffic in the same place. It seems that the area of pavement outside my house is home to a whole network of problematic utility pipes! Telecoms, drainage, cable television, street-furniture upgraders, all patiently take their turn at digging up the street. And then, because the surface of the road is now so poor and dangerous from all the patching up, the road resurfacers come and make it all neat and tidy again. A week or two later I open my curtains and there are the bollards and no-parking signs - again! I tried to find out exactly how many times the roads were dug up in my town, to no avail. But in Edinburgh the record stands at 11,500 times! How hard would it be for these disparate groups of road excavators to compare notes? Think of all the time and effort that could be saved.

It is easy to criticize (and we do!), but to what extent are our lives synchronized with the big picture? Is everything in order under the surface of our lives? Or do we try to sort out one mess one week, and then another mess another week, not realizing that everything is interconnected? Do we spend our lives patching up the holes? We make resolutions each New Year that get immediately broken, and then make the same resolutions the next year. We go on diets, budgets and health drives, only

I think I am a broken person. I seriously question the road my life has taken and I endlessly rehash the compromises I have made in my life.

Douglas Coupland

to fall back into our bad habits. We study to pass exams, and then forget what it was we used to be so good at. We make plans for our life, and then new plans, but if God the creator's plans are entirely different, it is like trying to build sandcastles against the incoming tide.

Some people look at the messiness of the world and deduce that there can be no God. We might think we are looking at the big picture, but in fact our vision is so limited that we can't see the big picture. We are like caterpillars inching our way across a billboard. We are so close to the subject matter that we can't get enough perspective to understand where the minuscule fraction of reality we can see fits into the greater whole. Imagine a rock climber working his way up the Statue of Liberty - he is so concerned about footholds and grips that he can't make out the facial features. Perhaps the mess we see up close looks different from another perspective.

In order to get a handle on the big picture of history we need another angle. The Bible tells the story of the life of our universe in big and broad brushstrokes. We have seen how the early chapters explain why we are here, and why we experience such a mixture of pleasure and pain. But is there anything else that points to God's purposes for us now?

My wife's family were big fans of the Inspector Morse series on television. In the old days of videotape they would record every episode and watch the programme all over again, looking for clues they'd missed. Marrying into such a family, I did my job as a dutiful son-in-law and sat and watched with them and pretty soon I was hooked too. So you can imagine that the last episode of Inspector Morse was a momentous event for us. My highlight was waiting to find out whether there would be a guest appearance by Morse's creator, Colin Dexter, who had made cameo appearances in all but three of the previous thirty-two episodes. It was a sad and serious episode as Morse faced death. So how did he relate to his creator on screen? Were there words of remorse or words of advice? Was there warmth? No. There was nothing of consequence.

If our creator wrote himself into the story of his creation, when would he appear? What would he do? What would we say to each other? Would it be a highly significant moment of history or an inconsequential non-event? Christians believe Jesus' arrival in the world was a momentous occasion, as the Author joined in the story of history. The clocks were set to zero, and the dating system recalibrated. Jesus did not come as a walk-on extra, to experiment in engaging in the trivialities of life. When Jesus came to earth he brought with him a message so radical it turned the world upside down. This message answers the question: What on earth is going on? But to understand it fully, we need to see it in perspective. We need to go back to the beginning of the Bible, step back as far as possible and look at the big picture.

A New Hope

When Adam and Eve took the forbidden fruit, God could have rightfully ended history right there and then. If God had treated the creation of the world like a game or an experiment, he could have just wrapped things up before they got any more complicated, and started again. Adam and Eve 2 – The Sequel, or Adam and Eve Reloaded! This would probably have been our inclination. When things are broken we are tempted to throw them away, whether a mobile phone or a relationship, and start again. But God doesn't give up. He has a plan.

The ground rules had been made very clear. If anyone ate from the tree of the knowledge of good and evil there would be death. God was not bluffing. The offending couple are banished from the garden, separated from God, alienated from each other, and made mortal. But, in the middle of the judgement, there is mercy.

> *So the LORD God said to the serpent, "Because you have done this, cursed are you above all the livestock and all the wild animals! You will crawl on your belly and you will eat dust all the days of your life. And I will put enmity between you and the woman, and between your offspring and hers; he will crush your head, and you will strike his heel."*
>
> *To the woman he said, "I will greatly increase your pains in childbearing; with pain you will give birth to children. Your desire will be for your husband, and he will rule over you."*
>
> *To Adam he said, "Because you listened to your wife and ate from the tree about which I commanded you, 'You must not eat of it', cursed is the ground because of you; through painful toil you will eat of it all the days of your life. It will produce thorns and thistles for you, and you will eat the plants of the field. By the sweat of your brow you will eat your food until you return to the ground, since from it you were taken; for dust you are and to dust you will return."*
>
> *(Genesis 3:14-19)*

A Matter of Life and Death

God spells out the consequences of their betrayal. These were the consequences he was trying to protect them from when he set the ground rules in the first place.

But even in the reading-out of their sentences there is hope. Although death is coming, there will first be new life. God tells Adam and Eve that they will have offspring and he tells the serpent that this offspring will one day overcome the forces of evil.

God declares that a rescuer is coming, a rescuer who will once and for all crush the head of the serpent. Through the generations that followed, God's people kept a lookout for this serpent-crusher. Would it be the immediate offspring of Adam and Eve - Cain or Abel? They turned out to be a murderer and his victim. Would it be a great Bible hero such as Abraham or Moses or Joshua or David or Solomon? All these people showed potential, but none of them was right. God kept promising a rescuer, and as history unfolded the details became clearer. This rescuer would be known as the Messiah; he would come from the ancestral line of King David; he would be a mighty leader; he would have a special relationship with God; he would be born in the town of Bethlehem.

Before we get ahead of ourselves, let's take one last look at chapter 3 of Genesis where there is another subtle clue in God's mercy to Adam and Eve:

> **The LORD God made garments of skin for Adam and his wife and clothed them.**
> **(Genesis 3:21)**

Expecting to be executed for their rebellion, they listen to God pronouncing the curses on them; and expecting death, they watch as he kills not them but some animals. The animals are killed for their skins, which are used for garments to cover up their embarrassment. This sacrifice is initiated by God within the garden of Eden, immediately after sin, to deal with the consequences of rebellion. This idea of sacrifice has powerful connections right through the Bible.

Fast-forward a few generations and God chooses a couple of pensioners, Sarah and Abraham, to be the parents of a nation. This is such an unlikely prospect that Sarah herself bursts out laughing. Yet after all sorts of scrapes and adventures the promise comes true and Isaac is born. Of course, Abraham dotes on his long-awaited, beloved son. But one day God asks Abraham if he is willing to sacrifice him out of love for God. Imagine the heartache of a loving and elderly father. Abraham knows that he has to obey God. But before the boy can be harmed God provides a ram, which Abraham sacrifices in place of his precious son.

Fast-forward another couple of generations and God's people are slaves in Egypt. Moses, their representative, enters into an epic conflict with Pharaoh. Ten plagues ensue, and with each one Moses asks Pharaoh to release the Israelites. With each refusal the intensity of the plagues increases. The final plague is to be the worst: the eldest child in each household will die in the night at the hand of the angel of the Lord. The Israelites are told to sacrifice a lamb and paint its blood on the doorposts of their houses. This lamb will act as a substitute for the firstborn son.

Later, as Moses leads the Israelites from captivity to the freedom of the promised land, God initiates a system for dealing with the sin of the community. On the most holy day of the year, the Day of Atonement, the chief priest is to take a goat, put his hands on its head and confess the sins of the people. The scapegoat is then to be released into the desert to demonstrate that the animal is carrying their sins far away.

Fast-forward again. Animals were still being sacrificed in the Temple to symbolize cleansing from all sorts of sins. The Old Testament expected God's people to use the sacrificial system to represent forgiveness for sin, but by the end of this part of the Bible the prophets are speaking of the inadequacies of the system:

*He was rejected by God
so that we could be accepted by God.*

For I desire mercy, not sacrifice, and acknowledgment of God rather than burnt
offerings. Like Adam, they have broken the covenant - they were unfaithful to
me there. (Hosea 6:6)

Fast-forward another few hundred years and a wild Jewish teacher, the most respected spiritual man of his generation, was by the river in the desert. John was baptizing men and women in the river, symbolizing their desire to turn away from sin. He saw a young man approaching the crowd and identified him as "the lamb of God that takes away the sin of the world".[15]

There is a finality and a universality about this massive statement. John did not point to "a lamb" or "another lamb", but said most definitively that this person was the ultimate sacrificial lamb - the best and the last of the sin sacrifices. The young man, the Lamb of God, was born in the town of Bethlehem, was from the ancestral line of King David, and was to become a mighty leader, with a special relationship with God. This was Jesus, the Messiah, God's only Son, who was born to be sacrificed for the sin of humanity once and for all. Jesus was born to die. Finally, here is the serpent-crusher we have been waiting for.

The cross in the ancient world was as unthinkable as a corporate logo as it would be today. Compare it with the power and prestige that are implied by symbols such as the Nike "swoosh", the Mercedes "star" or the Puma "cougar". The cross, on the other hand, is a symbol of abject humiliation and excruciating torture. It represents the Roman authorities' favourite method of torturing those foolish enough to challenge their military might. Yet the cross is the most widely recognized symbol of the Christian faith.

The four biographies of Jesus that we are given in the Bible leave us in no doubt as to what Jesus' life was about. They cover thirty years of Jesus' life at breakneck speed. Reading the Gospels is like watching a DVD at 20x speed. But when it comes to the last week of Jesus' life, suddenly the story goes into slow motion. The sacrifice of Jesus for sin on the cross is literally crucial for understanding God's plan for the earth.

The cross is an integration point at which we see most clearly what on earth God is doing. Not only is the cross the missing piece of the jigsaw, it also tackles the problem of missing peace due to the brokenness of the four relationships that we have looked at in the previous chapters. It offers both hope and a chance for our life to be synchronized with God's big picture. Through his death and his life, Jesus began a process of restoring the four ruptured relationships.

SPIRITUAL

Jesus came into our world, with its mixture of beauty and beastliness, untainted by the infection of sin. Just as the serpent accosted the first perfect human beings to walk the face of the earth, the devil also accosts Jesus. He feeds him the same lies and deceptions he fed to Adam and Eve at the beginning of time. Jesus was vulnerable.

He was in a desert, not a garden.

He was alone, not with a soulmate.

He was starving hungry, not well fed.

He was tempted at least three times – not once. Adam and Eve succumbed. Jesus resisted.

Jesus, as he lived the daily struggle of life, did not betray God. In fact, his life on earth displayed an unprecedented intimacy with God the Father. Through private meditation, public prayer and a common purpose he was always online with God. Jesus not only demonstrated a perfect peaceful relationship with God, he bought back that privilege for us through his death. He removed our sins from us when he died on the cross as a perfect sacrifice. Now we can be restored again to those perfect relationships that were planned from the beginning of history.

As Jesus hung on the cross he willingly took the punishment for the sins of the world. As Jesus cried out that he had been forsaken by his Father, the sky turned black, as though God were blocking the view. Jesus was forsaken by God so that we could be forgiven by God. He was rejected by God so that we could be accepted by God.

At the moment of Jesus' death the curtain that separated the Holy of Holies from the rest of the Temple was miraculously torn in two from top to bottom. To understand the significance of this we need to understand that God originally initiated the Temple system to provide a tangible place for his people to be with him. The inner sanctum, the Holy of Holies, was off limits. This signified that God's direct presence was so pure that impure human beings needed to be protected from him. Once a year the chief priest was allowed into this holiest place, and even then only after significant sacrifices and thorough ceremonial washing. As the curtain ripped from top to bottom, God showed that Jesus' death brought free access to him without the need for the sacrifices and the ceremonies. To the Jews this was as unthinkable as it would be for us to offer guided tours to the centre of a nuclear reactor without providing protective clothing. God's moral requirements have been met; his presence is now freely available, and spiritual intimacy is restored.

Of course a divided curtain, darkness and the death of a man does not prove that we can have peace with God. If the cross had been the end of Jesus, then Christianity would never have got started, let alone made such an impact on the world.

Jesus died from suffocation, and a Roman soldier speared his side to make doubly sure he was dead. That soldier was thorough. He would have faced stiff penalties for failing the standard of expert public execution. Jesus' lifeless body was taken away and buried in the donated family tomb of a wealthy man. The religious leaders of the time feared the theft of the body and the stories that might circulate, so they requested a Roman guard to be put on the tomb. All seems to have gone well for those who had plotted this operation. Jesus was dead, his followers scattered or in hiding, and Christianity was over before it could begin. Nevertheless, three days later the tomb is empty; the guards have vanished. Jesus' followers are suddenly transformed, out of hiding and willing to face imprisonment, ostracism and death. They claim to have seen and talked with Jesus, alive again. Jesus' death bought us peace with God. Jesus' resurrection proves it. It reveals that all his claims were true.

The implications for us are huge and life-changing. Jesus offers us the gift of perfect relationship with God because he took our sins away with his sacrifice. We can experience some of this on earth as we follow Jesus' example of being permanently connected with God, our Father. We will experience it fully as we follow Jesus through death and out the other side. If we choose to align the purpose of our life on earth with God's purposes, we can accept this incredibly generous offer of forgiveness, a clean slate and an untainted spiritual relationship with God.

RELATIONAL

As well as reconciliation with God, Jesus' death also offers hope for our interpersonal relationships. The whole world longs to hear this good news. Films and novels offer us heroes and heroines who live happily ever after. Magazines direct us to self-appointed lifestyle experts to help us. But the celebrities show us that, for all their wealth and beauty and access to experts around the world, they struggle to keep their marriages together, to keep their children off drugs and to retain their friendships. The strains are common to all of us, famous or otherwise. And if we struggle to keep it together with people that share our DNA, postcodes and languages, what hope is there for a fragmented world? Where will we find the resources to make peace in the Middle East or to bring equality between rich and poor, or to stop the ethnic cleansings?

Jesus is the peacemaker par excellence. His hand-picked disciples represented a complete cross-section of society. They were natural enemies brought together in friendship. Simon was a former terrorist who sought to wreak havoc against the occupying Roman forces. Levi was from the opposite extreme of the political spectrum; he was a collaborator with the Romans, doing their dirty work collecting inflated taxes for the invading army. But Jesus makes peace as he unites these two men within his band of brothers who are willing to live and die for each other. Jesus makes peace as he challenges the battle of the sexes by giving public recognition and respect to women from all walks of life. Jesus makes peace as he relates to the poor, the socially excluded, the underclasses and the intellectuals. Jesus taught: "Blessed are the peacemakers, for they shall be called sons of God."[16] As the Son of God himself, he had this family trait in full measure.

Although Jesus' peacemaking life made him many enemies, his peacemaking death made God available for everybody. As we understand this transformational reconciliation, the differences that arise between us and others become inconsequential. Following Jesus means following his example to bring peace to those around us, whatever the cost. As Jesus was dying on the cross he was thinking not about himself, but about others. He offered his fellow death-row convict peace with God. He offered his own mother a secure future as he called out to her and his friend John to care for each other as mother and son. Jesus' death models the love and care necessary for fulfilled human relationships on an individual level.

At the moment of Jesus' death the curtain separating us from God was torn down. According to the apostle Paul, whose letters are recorded in the Bible, another piece of metaphorical demolition work was also going on in the Temple at that moment. The problems of accessibility in the Temple that separated Jews from non-Jews were also torn down, showing that ethnicity did not matter to God. Jesus' death models love and peace at an interracial level.

ENVIRONMENTAL

Adam and Eve were tempted by the serpent to eat fruit in a lush garden filled with everything they could ever want. They fell for it, and the environment they were supposed to rule over and care for began to disintegrate around them. Jesus was tempted by the devil to turn rocks into bread after he had been fasting in the desert for forty days. By refusing to obey the devil, he wins the battle to rule creation that Adam and Eve lost so miserably. When Jesus does create bread, he miraculously turns it into a feast for 5,000. He turns mud into balm for the blind. He stills storms

"Christz says... I'm not saying I'm a teacher. I'm not saying
I'm a prophet. I'm saying:'I'm the Messiah'. I'm saying;'I',
am God incarnate...' Either Christ was who He said He was
– the Messiah - or a complete nutcase."

Bono

with a few words. He instructs professional fishermen where to find the best catch. He walks on water. There is no doubt when Jesus is around that he is ruling over creation, not to exploit it, but for the benefit of humans and for the glory of God. The regeneration project of the planet has begun.

When Jesus is executed, he is nailed onto a tree that he made, by people he had created. But Jesus was not being ruled by creation. By allowing himself to be the perfect sacrificial lamb for the sin of the world, he is inflicting defeat on the devil. It seems that Jesus is being destroyed, but in fact it is just a superficial blow - like the strike to the heel mentioned in Genesis 3. All that is left after the death and resurrection are the scars on Jesus' hands and feet. Jesus has the upper hand. As for the devil, Jesus struck a crushing blow to his head, ending his hold on planet earth.

PERSONAL

We are told that Jesus had no earthly beauty that would draw us to him. We know he was considered to be illegitimate and that he was born into a marginal tribe in a marginal town. His national identity gave no pride as the land was under the rule of the Roman Empire. Jesus was disliked by the authorities and deserted by his friends. Yet Jesus did not have a problem with self-image. His relationship to the Father was enough for him. Jesus knew who he was and what he was about. He was a man on a mission and refused to be blown off course by the crowds, the devil, his close friends, or even his own desires. Jesus' imminent death did not make his life meaningless. On the contrary: Jesus was born to die, and through his death he bought back the peace of the world. Lost identity and frustrated self-image can begin to be rehabilitated back to their former beauty.

When we look at ourselves, we know that we often feel ashamed and unworthy. But Jesus through his death on the cross bought us a peace that enables us to see ourselves in a new light. The thief hanging on the cross next to Jesus faced reality and realized that his punishment was fair. He feared God, and knew that his only hope was to beg Jesus for mercy. He had no way or time to make things good for himself. As he put his trust in a dying man's promise, he knew that he could face death with the imminent hope of paradise.

You Only Live Twice

It is difficult for us to fully grasp the big picture that the Bible describes. God in the middle of our history sent a second Adam to repair the damage the original Adam had caused. That second Adam, Jesus, did the repair work necessary, and also showed us how to live our life in line with God's big picture of restoration, reconciliation, regeneration and rehabilitation.

In the place where God has put us, we are called to live in intimacy with God. We are sent to be peacemakers in the world, ruling over creation as we resist the temptations of the devil. We are no longer afraid of death, but embrace it as the gateway to paradise. The only way we can do this is to follow Jesus. We need to trust him as the thief on the cross did, to provide us with peace with God and with the hope of heaven. We must follow his example of shunning selfish social norms and relating to people across the spectrum and across the globe.

If you have never done this before, take time to consider yourself realistically. Perhaps you can admit that you are not at peace with God, other people, yourself or the environment. Talk to God about falling short of his standards, and ask him for mercy. Thank him for the forgiveness and peace he offers you through what Jesus did in his life and death. Ask him to help you live your life in line with his purposes for the world. Trust him to bring you to paradise after you die.

This chapter has been a whistle-stop tour of the big picture of the history of the planet, as described in the Bible. We can see from our diagram that, because of Jesus, the four relationships are beginning to be repaired. Christians claim that by following Jesus we can choose to be part of the process of restoration, reconciliation, regeneration and rehabilitation. But the story is not over yet. We still need to find out how we can make sense of this as we look at our everyday lives. We still need to find out whether it will all be worth it in the end.

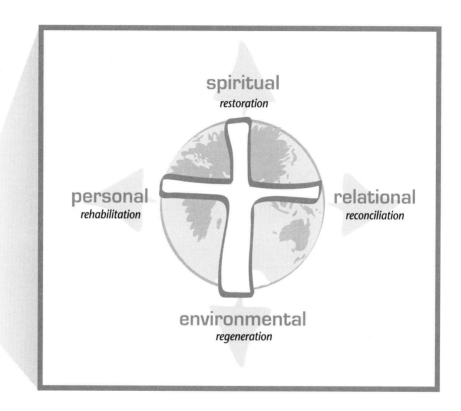

5

Which way should I go?

Who Dares Wins

I was sure I was going to win. After all, when you are ten it is normal to assume you are going to win every competition you enter. The prize would be a dream come true: a five-minute shopping spree in an HMV store where I could fill my shopping trolley to the brim with prizes. I planned every detail, not wanting to waste a millisecond. I knew where I would start, what I would grab, and how I would maximize the space in my trolley. I used to lie awake planning it, and when I did fall asleep, it was just to wake again in a cold sweat facing the nightmare that I had lost my store map and was trapped in the country-music section!

I thought about this the other day when I was in Blackwell's in Oxford, Europe's largest bookshop. It stocks over 250,000 titles. If I am lucky I manage a book a week. Even if I managed a book a day it would take me 684 years to read all the books. That's without reckoning on the fact that every year there are thousands of new books being printed. So I must choose the books I want to read very carefully. Similarly, my online DVD company has over 60,000 titles in its database. At a film a day I would only make it through that catalogue in 164 years! I love films and so must choose the ones I watch wisely. Faced by such a vast choice I am painfully aware of my own finitude.

I am still waiting for the phone call that will let me know that they have found my winning entry into the HMV trolley sweep - twenty-five years too late! But as I carry on dreaming about how to make the most out of those elusive 300 seconds, or the most of my choice of books and DVDs this week, I reflect on my attitude towards the rest of my life. How will I plan my route? How will I decide what is the most important and most valuable use of the time I have left? Or will I just drift along thinking I have all the time in the world?

Helen Quilley has had a terrible day; she has lost her job, and walks dejectedly onto the platform to catch the underground home only to find that she has missed the Tube by seconds. She arrives home late and gets a small measure of sympathy from her boyfriend.

Helen Quilley has had a terrible day; she has lost her job, and walks dejectedly onto the platform, just squeezing through the sliding doors onto the Tube. She arrives home to find her boyfriend in bed with another woman. She ends their relationship on the spot and storms out of the house.

These are the opening sequences of a film called Sliding Doors. There is a split-second difference between the two scenarios in which Helen either just catches or just misses the train. This split-second difference opens up two completely different courses for her life.

Friends of mine realized the serious point that the film was making when they went in to work in London on 7 July 2005. Both of them narrowly missed taking the train that was blown up at Aldgate. Perhaps one had decided to stop to buy a newspaper; perhaps the other had decided on the shorter queue at the ticket office, which had inevitably ended up being slower than the longer queue! It appears that the very small, seemingly insignificant decisions we make in life can have a huge impact on our destiny.

Have you ever been lost and asked for directions, only to be given the nonsensical reply: "I'm sorry; you can't get there from here"? I am truly surprised how often people say that. We have seen how important it is to make sure our life ambitions match God's plan for the planet. But how do we get there from here? Every day throws decisions at us. We need help with the big choices, such as what to study, what career to choose, and whether to marry or have children. We also need help with the smaller choices, such as what to buy at the supermarket, what to prioritize at work, and which of our friends to keep in touch with. If small factors can make such a big difference, we need help every second of our lives.

How we tackle choices shows up who we really are. Decision-making shows our true colours. We may say we believe something, but we demonstrate what we truly value in the decisions we make. We may believe we are concerned for the environment, but if we live in a city and drive a gas-guzzling off-roader, then the chances are that we are not really that concerned about our carbon footprint.

Many of us hate making decisions and so often put them off for as long as possible. A decision can feel like closing down the possibilities. The postponement method often means that people get married later, have children later in life, change careers several times in their lifetime, and never get around to finishing books or filling in a tax return. The delay tactic allows us to be free of making decisions in life, as the decisions are often made for us if we just wait long enough.

At the opposite end of the spectrum, some people tackle the decision-making process by becoming control freaks. They are the sort of people who are so scared of waiting for somebody else to make a decision that they jump in and make it for them. They know exactly what coffee to buy at Starbucks before they have even gone through the front door. They always take charge of the remote control and often finish your sentences! They seem to thrive on being decisive about every irrelevance in life.

And for anyone who needs to make decisions and can't, there is usually an expert out there somewhere. We are experts at looking for experts to help us decide. Independent financial advisors, life coaches and web reviews claim to take the stress out of our options. But the experts often just add to the stress. Perhaps there are too many of them. If you are struggling with a new baby, there is no need to fear. Just walk down the street and you will be told to keep her warm, cool her down, breastfeed, bottle-feed, put on her shoes, take her shoes off, feed her when she wants it, feed her when you want it, and so it goes on. We can be very opinionated when it comes to other people's lives, but very indecisive in our own. This seems to be especially true in the areas that really matter.

Dazed and Confused

In a world of information overload and a plethora of options, how do we develop the wisdom we need to make right decisions? If there is no God, some would say that decision-making doesn't really matter, because nothing really matters in the grand scheme of things as there is no grand scheme. Others would say that, if there is no God, then decision-making is the most important thing we can do because it is all we can do. They say we are defined by our decisions. Unfortunately, we cannot know the consequences of many of our decisions, so we have to make them blind. I heard the story of a man who decided not to wear a jacket to work. The weather turned cold and the next day he woke up with the 'flu.

The beautiful new administrator who arrived in the office that day accepted a date with the man's colleague and a year later was married to him. The man forever looked at that couple and regretted his decision to leave his jacket at home.

Considering a biblical approach to decision-making acts as a window through which to see whether the Christian faith makes any practical difference to everyday life. Christianity offers an alternative view of decision-making to those we have looked at so far. The Bible makes it clear that God guides his people. He is described as a perfect father who wants the best for his children. He is described as a shepherd that leads his flock to quiet waters and lush grazing. He is described as the creator who knows how we were designed to live life to the full. At one level, choosing to follow the guidance of the creator of the world makes perfect sense. It is as logical as consulting the manual when we are trying to work out how to use our new DVD recorder. We have also seen that God shows his genuine love for us by sacrificing his own Son in our place. This provides a strong basis for us to trust that his guidelines for life will be in our best interests. In fact, even the most selfish person in the world should listen to God's guidance, as it is going to be the best thing for him or her!

Some people assume that if God guides he must have a specific plan for the life of each of us. They assume that God has already preordained whether or whom we are to marry, which house we are supposed to live in and the work colleagues, holidays and grandchildren we are supposed to have. This view of guidance feels a little like a narrow mountain path: there is just one specific route we need to take from cradle to grave. Anything off this path is wrong, or second best. There are many problems with this view. How do we find out what that plan is? What if we inadvertently step off course? What if we got some inconsequential decision

wrong, and caught a train with a bomb on it? What if we marry the wrong person, buy the wrong house, or accept the wrong job? Are we bound to live a life that has no significance? Are we stuck with Plan B?

Before Sunrise

The Bible has some examples of very clear and specific guidance. For instance, Joseph is told to marry Mary (in a dream), Abraham is told to move house (by an angel), and Moses is called to change career (by a burning bush). The problem is not that God chooses to guide in this way, but that we often anticipate that we are all going to be guided in this way all the time.

The isolated rural villages of northern Albania in the 1990s made me think of Israel in biblical times. Barefoot boys would sit in fields under the olive trees, watching herds of sheep. Farmers on donkeys would work the land with basic tools, and the women would sweep the whitewashed houses with brooms made of bunches of sticks. A friend of mine told me a story about a new Christian who been learning part of the story of Gideon at his church. It was the account of Gideon's test of God, in which Gideon sought clarity from God as to whether he really wanted him to lead an army against the invading Midianites. He laid down his sheepskin outside his house and asked that overnight God would cause the ground, but not the fleece, to be wet with dew. When this actually happened, he wanted to double-check, so he did a negative test sample, asking that God would cause the fleece, not the ground, to be damp from dew. God did this too, and Gideon was satisfied that he was acting according to God's will. So this friend of my friend, who also had a decision to make, used Gideon as a role-model and laid out his sheepskin overnight. He woke up expecting to find a miracle and the answer to his dilemma.

But he found neither. In fact, he did not even find his sheepskin! He thought he was discerning the will of God, but really he was just donating his fleece to the local black market! He learned a valuable (if expensive!) lesson about being careful how we read the stories in the Bible. They are not all supposed to act as examples for us to follow. But if this level of guidance is not available to us at every decision we make, what do we do when faced with a choice?

Another model of guidance is the opposite of the narrow path. It is an open football field. Imagine you have made it into the team and you are on the pitch. There are clear boundaries marked around the pitch. These white lines do not restrict play but actually make the game possible in the first place. There are rules. Don't pick up the ball (unless you are the goalkeeper). Use your legs to run. Don't bring a Sherman tank onto the pitch! But within those rules there is a great deal of flexibility. In fact, within these simple boundaries there is still an almost infinite amount of room for creativity. Rather than waiting for specific instructions every second of the game, good players get on and use their initiative, aware of other players around them, communicating with them and making wise choices for the benefit of the whole team. Moreover the manager does sometimes shout instructions and so the players need to keep an ear open to specific directions as and when they come.

I like the football analogy! I like the fact that we can learn from previous heroes of the game. I like the idea that we had an ultimate substitute who took the ultimate penalty for us and defeated the worst opposition we have ever had to face. But before I take my eye off the ball, we need to see how this might work out in practice and the best way is to return to our four relationships!

SPIRITUAL

When I was ten years old I was out at the shops trying to find my mum a present for Mother's Day. Things were not going well. Mum already had more flowers than would fit into our tiny garden. She had had Elizabeth Shaw mints from me for the last nine years. I needed a better idea. How hard could it be? I know my mum, I know what she likes and I know what makes her smile. So although there were no written instructions, working out what to buy should have been relatively easy.

When we have a relationship with God, we get to know him and we get to know what he likes. Thinking of what we can give him to make him smile is true worship. We can do this with the everyday parts of our lives. We can do this when we decide what food products to eat, what career steps to take, or how much money to spend on a holiday.

The problem with my shopping dilemma as a ten-year-old was that there was another tug on my heart. Lionel Richie, then the coolest singer I knew, now the paragon of middle-of-the-road American manufactured muzak, had just released a new album. My mum had never expressed a dislike of Lionel's mellow tones, but on the other hand neither had she ever expressed any particular interest in his funky grooves. I liked it. I thought she should like it, so... I bought the album, wrapped it up and presented it to her on the big day. To my mum's eternal credit she smiled, gave me a big hug and expressed great appreciation for the gift. Did she ever play it? Well, the short answer is no. But I certainly did...

To be honest, many people have a similar approach. We say that we want to follow God but really we give God whatever we want to give him. We live our lives our way and then we tell God that it's all for him. Our daily decisions should be about learning how to please God with all that we do, say and think. It's writing God a blank cheque. It's about offering him the driving seat. Jesus was very clear that we are called to "love the Lord our God with all our heart, soul and mind". This means that we seek to please him with all that we are.

I have a friend who chose to change career to a less lucrative one, so she could please God through her gift of counselling. I have a friend who was able to bring up her children in difficult circumstances, motivated by her obvious desire to please God. Another friend decided to give the profits from his company to invest in helping AIDS orphans in Africa. Another left a comfortable job in North London to travel to South America and live and work in relative poverty. None of these people heard a direct voice from God. They were not simply obeying rules and regulations. They were living to please God, and their choices reflected that.

RELATIONAL

The football analogy sees each player as part of a team. This is how the Bible teaches that we are to see ourselves, except it uses a slightly different analogy – that of the body. As members of one body, we recognize our own unique gifts and abilities, but also those of others around us, and we work together. We work together as God directs us, as a manager arranging the attackers and defenders on the pitch. We need each other, we look out for each other, we suffer and rejoice together.

This is a far cry from the way that many people understand the church. Unfortunately, the church is often seen as a spectator sport in which a few people up the front do all the work and the rest of us watch on. But Christ calls all believers to be involved in the life of the church community and involved in God's

plans for the world. On a daily basis this means making choices for the pleasure of God and the benefit of the community.

We have mentioned before that Jesus deliberately draws disparate types of people together and enables them not only to get along but to love and care for each other. The Christian life affects life outside the church, as work colleagues, friends, family and neighbours relate together. Outside the church, we are called to follow Jesus and be peacemakers, bringing the peace of God into every area of life.

When we are making decisions, we must bear in mind the effect our decisions will have on those around us. Cutting back on our working hours may enable us to be more effective husbands and fathers. Choosing to hang around at work at the end of the day to meet deadlines may make us more trusted and valued colleagues. Choosing to prioritize others over ourselves may have a huge impact on decisions about our time management, our bank balance, and our lifestyle. Considering the impact of our lives on other people involves thinking globally and acting locally.

ENVIRONMENTAL

Our world is beginning to face up to the consequences of our decision-making in the past. Finally, issues such as extreme poverty in Africa, chemical and sugar overloads in our food products, and pollution through toxic waste dumps are beginning to hit the political agenda, and being a follower of Christ involves taking the initiative to care for God's world even in our basic decision-making, in ways such as reducing packaging, reusing when possible, and recycling whatever we can. It means taking responsibility for the influence that we exert through our spending power, our roles at work, our example to our children and our use of the ballot box. I have been challenged by friends who buy fairly traded refreshments for their workplaces and refuse to accept plastic bags, and who have downgraded the engine size of their cars or switched to ethical banking. As they help me see how I can better take care of the planet, together we can live according to God's original mandate.

PERSONAL

When I was growing up I prided myself on being at the cutting edge of information technology. I would normally be found on a Saturday afternoon experimenting with friends on their prized ZX81, the pinnacle of home-computer gadgetry. We once spent five hours typing pages of numbers into it that we found in a magazine. Finally, success! Our patient programming had paid off. If we pressed the "X" key, the letter "I" popped up and moved to the right of the screen. If we pressed the "Z" key it moved to the left. If we pressed the space bar then it would shoot a little arrow up to the top of the screen, and if we were skilful enough it might actually manage to hit the letter "O" that was mischievously floating around at the top of the screen. Five hours of hard labour produced a great game. Unfortunately, we had only twenty minutes to enjoy it before we had to get home for tea. We switched the computer off and left. Had we read the manual, we would have discovered that, if we had plugged a tape recorder into the machine, we could have played the game again the following Saturday without needing to spend another five hours copying in the machine code. If only we had read the manual!

We often live with regrets because we make our decisions without reference to the designer's instructions. Life is complex and we are confronted with so many options. We have already mentioned many of the practical lifestyle choices we are faced with on a daily basis, but we also face decisions that are tough and cause not a small amount of tension and heartache. Deciding between France and Holland for a summer camping holiday is a win-win decision, but sometimes we are faced with situations in which we feel we lose whatever path we choose. What do we do when we suspect our best friend's husband of having an affair? What do we do when we find serious financial discrepancies in our manager's report? What do we do when we find we are pregnant at university?

Into the tension of difficult decisions the Christian faith speaks. The designer who offers us guidance directs us not through dictator-style rules and regulations but through fatherly love and instruction. Far from neglecting us and leaving us to fend for ourselves, God provides a framework for decision-making with clear boundaries and room for freedom. God provides us in his Son with a perfect living example who faced a whole lifetime of difficulties. God offers us his Spirit inside us to give us the strength we need to make the tough decisions and to walk with us through the challenges of life. God offers us forgiveness when we make the wrong decisions, and a clean slate to start afresh. God offers us the resources to be able to look at our past and learn from it. God offers us unswerving love and commitment through all the ups and downs of life.

Love Actually

The Bible is full of stories, examples and teaching that are appropriate to coping with what life throws at us. You would have to read it and study it for yourself to see the ways in which it can be applied to all our modern-day dilemmas. There are various books available to help you get started and your local church should be able to offer you not only some advice on this but live examples of people who glean help from God and each other in a practical and down-to-earth way.

I hope this brief look at decision-making has shown the practical difference that becoming a follower of Jesus actually makes to life today. This is vitally important because it affects one of the most important decisions in your life: whether to follow Jesus. And the decision is not just an intellectual one. In fact, it is similar to the decision to get married.

In one sense, getting married is the easiest thing in the world; it involves only four words: "I will" and "I do". But those four words have enormous implications. Marriage is neither a hobby nor a part-time affair. Marriage will affect your future, your money, your career, your whole life. No one should jump into marriage without the proper thought and consideration. Firstly, there are intellectual considerations: Is your fiancée already married? Is she a blood relative? Could I cope if she started to snore, squeeze the toothpaste in the middle or spend money like water? Could I stick with it if she lost her looks, if she got ill or if we can't have children? But most of these intellectual considerations can't be answered conclusively. I have to trust what I know of my fiancée and our relationship to reasonably assume that we can make it as a marriage partnership. It is similar with the Christian faith. We approach it intellectually but not all our questions can be answered conclusively. At some point we need to trust what we know of God's character.

On the eve of my wedding I felt all the normal emotional excitement of love and anticipation. But I knew that these feelings were not enough on their own to make our marriage work. I knew that bad news, bad weather and bad moods would banish any rush of gush. I also knew that if I felt nothing for my wife, the marriage would not work. As we discover more about Jesus, we are attracted to him. His ability to make the outcast feel special, to challenge the hypocrisy of the management and to bring the dead back to life rouses our emotions. It motivates us to follow him to the ends of the earth.

On my wedding day, I was not asked whether I had thought long and hard about my wife and our future marriage. I was not asked how I felt about her. I was asked:

> *Will you have this woman as your wife? Will you love her, cherish her, honour and protect her, in sickness and in health; and, forsaking all others, be faithful to her, as long as you both shall live?*

The question is not addressed to my intellect or my emotions, but to my will. It is a decision about commitment. Following Jesus is a promise of commitment. Will you love the Lord your God with all your heart, soul and mind, and will you love your neighbour as yourself?

This chapter has shown what answering these questions with "I do" could look like in practice on a day-to-day basis. This is one of the biggest decisions of your life. It will affect everything about you. Nobody will force you to make the decision; it is yours alone to make. It is worth taking some time to consider the choice and the implications.

This chapter has also offered a model for all our other decisions in life. By returning to our diagram, we can see that we need to check each decision against our four key relationships. Are we pleasing God? Are we prioritizing the needs of others? Are we protecting the environment? Are we preserving our own consciences?

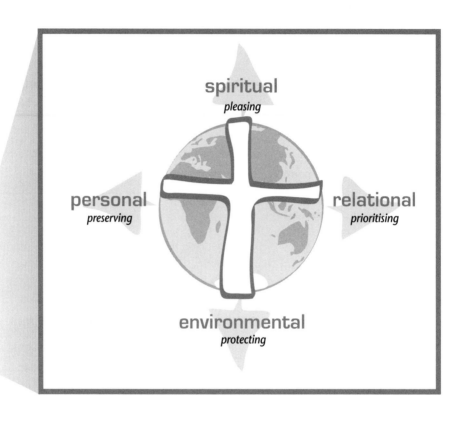

6

Where is my life going?

Planes, Trains and Automobiles

It is too late, you are trapped. Maybe it has happened to

you. The first train was delayed and the time you have between trains has been reduced considerably! You dash off, trying to remember all your belongings, and scan the platforms and display boards for any information about your next train. You look around for anyone in uniform, and then jump onto the train you believe to be yours. Relieved, you sit down in the first available seat, just as the doors lock and the train pulls away from the platform. As the tannoy mumbles something about somewhere, a panicky thought flashes across your mind, and you blurt out to your calm fellow passenger, who is reading a newspaper or knitting: "This is the train to Birmingham New Street, isn't it?" Of course, by this point, it doesn't really matter what the answer is. You are on that train, and there is nothing you can do about it. If you have inadvertently caught the wrong connection, you are trapped travelling in the wrong direction. Neither panicking nor knitting will do anything to change the destination. It is too late.

This is a dangerous place to be in if this is your life story. You may think you are travelling in one direction, but if you have never taken the time to consider checking the final destination, you could be seriously mistaken.

For many people, life is a runaway train, with no brakes and no controls. It rushes on into the future at an unstoppable pace. The days seem to pass by in a blur, the birthdays coming round at an increasing rate. Life can be like the movie Speed. In this film, Sandra Bullock just happens to be a passenger on a bus that has had a bomb planted on it. The evil genius has designed the bomb to explode if the speed of the bus drops below fifty miles an hour. This causes havoc on the busy city streets of Los Angeles. Bullock's plucky but frantic character, trying to decide where to steer this bus so she doesn't kill herself, the passengers or the people on the streets, shot her to immediate stardom. Many of us can relate to the picture of her hanging on to the steering wheel for dear life as the bus thunders on. Our life is lived at a frenetic speed. We can't slow it down. All we can do is hang in there and try not to smash into anything as we push forward. Our lives often feel as if our foot is welded to the accelerator. Bullock eventually manages to get the bus to an airfield, where there is sufficient space to go round in circles without fear of knocking anyone over. Maybe that is why many of us have settled for the routines we are locked into. It's the way that we have learned to deal with the speed of life: go round in circles and avoid making decisions or facing the big question of where life is going.

Final Destination

There are some movies that should not be shown on a flight, and Final Destination is one of them! The film plays on the fears that many of us have about flying. The movie's hero is sitting on a 747 with his classmates, about to taxi onto the runway for take-off. He gets an alarming glimpse of the future and bolts for the door of the plane, taking as many of his friends as possible with him. As the plane climbs into the sky above the airport, those on the ground see it burst into flames - everyone is lost. The film follows those that survived as death hunts them down one by one. The film-makers delight in finding unusually gruesome ways of killing off the teenagers, through set-piece combinations of unlikely events - a dripping tap and a poorly insulated tanning bed, a roller coaster and a missing bolt. This film has an uncanny ability to use everyday objects to frighten us silly. The Final Destination web page had the cheerful title "Deathiscoming.com", and originally had a counter that showed how many people had died during the time you were browsing the site. It was an unlikely box-office hit, but it did well enough for the producers for it to warrant two sequels.

I was on a plane recently, trying not to think about Final Destination! I was worried about making sure that my new laptop was secure, my phone was in sight, my iPod was plugged in and my passport was safely out of reach. Halfway through the flight, the seatbelt signs came on. The captain announced that we would be experiencing some turbulence. Everyone was calm during the routine shaking, although admittedly I was still thinking about that new laptop in the luggage rack above my head. But, as the pitching and rolling became more intense, I couldn't even hold my coffee without spilling it. I looked around at the still-smiling cabin crew for some comfort, on whose foreheads were appearing faint beads of sweat! Most people on the plane were probably praying at that moment. I instantly stopped worrying about my computer, passport and phone. I began to ask God to take care of my wife and children. When life seems fragile it is the people in our lives that matter the most. The rest of the time we often forget about death, God, prayer and relationships and become distracted with gadgets and things. The distraction is welcome because facing death is not a subject we like to dwell on.

I was caught off guard once when an insurance salesman sat in my kitchen and asked me to draw a line that represented my life. He zoomed in on the end of the line and drew a big "X" and asked me how much thought I had given to my funeral arrangements and how my family would cope financially without me. I didn't invite him in for coffee again! Nobody likes to think about death.

Back to the Future

Paul McCartney penned a wonderful song about the future. He wrote it when the Beatles were at their zenith, in 1967, and it is on arguably their finest album, Sgt Pepper's Lonely Hearts Club Band. Paul was only twenty-five years old when he wrote *When I'm 64*. Nevertheless, he knew what was important to him and sang to us of his dream of growing old with someone. He wondered whether he would still be loved even when he lost his looks, teeth and hair! But Paul's first wife died of cancer, and he separated from his second wife in the year of his sixty-fourth birthday. Who would have thought that the voice behind the greatest rock band in the world, and a man with the world at his feet in 1967, would be alone on his sixty-fourth birthday? The dream of a bright future goes hand in hand with the fear of a bleak future, and the fear of death itself.

None of us when we are twenty-five knows what the future will be like. So, rather than consider our future and face our mortality, we focus on the present and adopt the "eat, drink and be merry" lifestyle while we can. Companies often focus on immediate profits rather than long-term investments. Our own financial planning often has a spend-today-worry-about-paying-for-it-tomorrow aspect. Fast-food restaurants work on the same principle: enjoy the quick fix of sugar, salt and fat now and don't think about the long-term dietary consequences. Up until recently we have had the same approach to the environment. We have burnt our way through fossil fuels, cut down rainforests and paved through countryside without much concern for the world we are leaving to our children.

Another way to avoid thinking about the future is to live in the past. I enjoy listening to our elderly friends talk about the good old days when gay meant happy, a joint was something that you cooked in the oven on Sundays, a date could be found only in the calendar, and a Macintosh was something you wore on a rainy day. Some have said that nostalgia isn't what it used to be, but in fact nostalgia is no longer aimed at the older generation but at me! The songs I loved when I was a kid are being re-released, and I am the target audience. The film producers are also targeting my generation when they bring out new Star Wars episodes, or films based on old TV shows such as Starsky and Hutch or The Dukes of Hazzard. I took my kids to see The Magic Roundabout when that came out, but they had no idea who Zebedee was! The film was just an excuse for me to remember my youth! If we don't avoid the future by thinking about the present, we are legitimately able to avoid the future by thinking about the past and embracing retro-culture. Unfortunately, the rewind button for life does not work. At best we can enjoy a few snatched freeze-frame images. The future is calling us.

Rather than facing the future, our hope-less culture hides from it in nostalgia or buries itself in the present. We lock ourselves into cyclical routines just as we see history as an endless repetition going nowhere (but maybe getting faster). In this book we have started to see the alternative view of history that the Bible has to offer. The Bible teaches that history has a definite beginning with the creation of a perfect world in which everything was rightly related. We saw that critical moment in history when rebellion led to ruptured relationships. We saw that central and crucial point of history when Jesus, God's Son, died. That was when the rescue plan for restoration began. We saw the accompanying event of history when Jesus was raised from the dead, giving a true hope to all those who follow him. That hope was and still is infectious and indestructible. Christians throughout the centuries

"The present is never our end. The past and the present are our means, the future alone is our end. Thus we never actually live, but hope to live, and since we are always planning how to be happy, it is inevitable that we never should be."

Blaise Pascal

have been willing to face family persecution, religious exclusion, verbal abuse, physical torture and martyrdom. They have been seized by the truth that Christ was alive, and the rightful King of the universe. But the story is not over yet. The Bible tells of another definite moment of time when the world as we know it will come to an end.

There is a famous image of Neville Chamberlain stepping off a plane on 30 September 1938. Then prime minister of Britain, he triumphantly and proudly waved a piece of paper, which guaranteed peaceful settlements to any disputes between Britain and Germany and an end to the fear of war. Anyone recording the post-World-War-One period as it occurred would have seen that moment as hugely significant. They might even have chosen to end their book on that decisive note, holding Neville Chamberlain up as one of Britain's most brilliant leaders. However, what happened in the following weeks changed everybody's view of Neville Chamberlain. As World War Two broke out, he went down in history as one of Britain's most foolish leaders, stupidly believing he could trust the word of Adolf Hitler.

With twenty-twenty hindsight, we have the benefit of making some judgement on our history. But it is very hard to work out what is really significant until the end of the story is known. Since history is not over yet, we may end up making exactly the same mistake again, deciding what is important before the story ends.

The greatest films are those that you want to watch again. When you get to the end, you realize that, as well as the twists, the director had built in a series of clues. They just seemed like a whole lot of seemingly unimportant details the first time round. Think of movies like *The Sixth Sense* or *The Usual Suspects*.

Knowing the future can help us work out what is ultimately important for life right now and help us to make wise decisions. The Bible shows us a picture of the end point of time, when history will be wrapped up. This picture leaves us in no doubt as to where the train of life is heading:

> ***Then I saw a new heaven and a new earth, for the first heaven and the first earth had passed away, and there was no longer any sea. I saw the Holy City, the new Jerusalem, coming down out of heaven from God, prepared as a bride beautifully dressed for her husband. And I heard a loud voice from the throne saying, "Now the dwelling of God is with men, and he will live with them. They will be his people, and God himself will be with them and be their God. He will wipe every tear from their eyes. There will be no more death or mourning or crying or pain, for the old order of things has passed away."***
>
> ***He who was seated on the throne said, "I am making everything new!" Then he said, "Write this down, for these words are trustworthy and true." (Revelation 21:1-5)***

Here is God's picture of the end of time. In this picture we can see how each of the relationships we have been looking at through this book is worked out in the end.

SPIRITUAL

The book of Revelation is the record of a vision that John, one of Jesus' closest friends, had while in prison on the Greek island of Patmos. Revelation, although the cause of much debate, is a visual snapshot from the end of history in which we are given a vision of a heavenly city – a metropolis where God will live with humanity in a restored relationship. In fact, the divine-human relationship will be even better than the one described in Eden. There, God only came into the garden

The journey of humanity began in a garden.

It ends in a city.

to walk with humanity. Here, God will live together with his people for ever. The passage layers images on top of one another. The heavenly city is described as a bride dressed up on her wedding day. Just as a bride counts down the weeks and hours to the big day and prepares for it for months in advance, so this day will be the grand finale of all the preparations through history. Built into us is dissatisfaction with life and a longing for God that come with being made in his image. Our homesickness is finally removed when God comes to take up residence with his people.

This passage takes us on from the ripped curtain we saw in Chapter 4. The torn Temple curtain spoke of free access to the presence of God. John's vision shows there is no need for a Temple. God will manifest his presence everywhere. Elsewhere in Revelation, we are told that the heavenly city will have the dimensions of a perfect cube. It is no coincidence that in the temple, the Holy of Holies was also a perfect cube. God will live with his people in a new and tangible way.

At the beginning of time, we had a perfect relationship with God, but when rebellion occurred in Eden that relationship was damaged. Jesus came into the world to broker peace between God and humanity, but to many it seems as worthless as Neville Chamberlain's piece of paper. Just as some DVDs offer alternative endings, so the Bible also talks about an alternative future apart from God's presence. We need to take seriously our decision about whether or not to follow Jesus. The choice we make now will determine our final destination. We are still living in a time of spiritual searching and a fractious relationship with God. Only the end of the story will prove its reality, and according to the Bible we will not be disappointed. So in the meantime Christians live by faith that this peace is in fact effective and we trust Jesus' promises for the future.

RELATIONAL

The journey of humanity began in a garden. It ends in a city. In fact, the imagery of a city-bride is a powerful combination of relational metaphors. The city speaks of a community and a bride speaks of intimacy. Heaven will be a bustling metropolis; a cosmopolitan community living in close quarters. The idea of ending up in a city is a frightening prospect for many! We often dream about escaping to a place in the country where we can finally untangle our lives from the crowded hustle and bustle. We associate cities with ghettoes and slums and their related vices: graffiti, crime and disaffection. But the picture here is of that perfect peace that we looked at in Chapter 2. This time no imperfection is allowed anywhere near to corrupt or ruin the perfect community of God's people. There will be no more war, abuse, blame or divorce. The French philosopher Jean-Paul Sartre famously said "Hell is other people", but the Bible argues that it is heaven that is intimately connected with other people. The deepest joys in life connected with our relationships act like travel brochures, preparing us for the end of the journey.

Life in community is a taste of life to come. Because of this, throughout the centuries this vision of right human relationships has spurred Christians on to work for justice in the here and now. While civil war raged in Zimbabwe in the 1960s, students at Harare University were told to eat their meals at separate tables for blacks and whites. The Christians from the International Fellowship of Evangelical Students had other plans. The black and white Christian students sat and ate together. Not only that, the white students collected the main course and served it to their black brothers and sisters and then the black Christians served dessert to their white brothers and sisters.[17] These students were time travellers: they lived with one foot in the present and another in the heavenly city. They brought the values of God's future into the present. They wanted to visibly demonstrate where history was going. This same experience should be part of the life of the church every day. Church should not be a time machine taking us back into the Dark Ages, Middle Ages, Victorian England or even the good old 1980s! It should be a time machine taking us forward to a taste of the cosmopolitan city-bride community. Christians must be keen to work for social transformation. William Wilberforce and his team worked for 21 years to end the transatlantic slave trade. They wanted to demonstrate God's unconditional love for all people and to bring a taste of the heavenly city to today's world.

ENVIRONMENTAL

There are so many beautiful places on this planet. I remember taking a boat ride along the southern Albanian coast with friends. The sea was crystal blue and the summer sun felt good on our backs. We stopped off on an idyllic deserted island where we spent the day together, swimming, chatting and exploring. Later in the day the boatman dropped us off some tomatoes, feta cheese, fresh bread and chilled drinks. It felt as if we had been marooned in paradise. Later that same summer I took another group of friends to the same place, but it had been transformed. There was rubbish piled high along the beaches, broken bottles in the water, a distinct smell of urine. The paradise was lost. It was still a great place: blue sea, sand and shade – but it was a pale shadow of what it had once been.

Planet earth is in pretty much the same condition. It's a great place, but there's enough damage for us to know that it's not what it once was, nor what it ought to be. As we appreciate the amazing sunsets and the colours of the sea, we also ache when we see the destruction of the rainforests or the parched lands of the two-thirds world. This passage from Revelation shows us that one day everything will be sorted out. The new heavens and the new earth will be pristine and pure, as good as new. We long for the day when natural disasters will be a thing of the past, when our children can play out safely, when the basic necessities of food and water will be fairly distributed. This passage flags up the restoration of the planet. Elsewhere the Bible speaks of the lion lying down with a lamb, and a boy putting his hand into the nest of snakes and not getting bitten. The new heaven and earth will be perfectly safe and perfectly peaceful.

A better world is coming, but this doesn't mean a licence to rape the soil and scorch the skies. Instead, knowing we will be held accountable for how we have used the resources of the planet, we are challenged to provide a taste of that future now. Repainting a post-communist orphanage, clearing rubbish from a local park, campaigning for governments to take climate change seriously, or taking housebound pensioners to a rose garden are all ways in which others can be given a taste of the future hope.

PERSONAL

Cinderella Man was one of those films I shouldn't have enjoyed watching! Another heroic role for Russell Crowe, this time playing the legendary boxer Jim Braddock. Braddock, with a promising career ahead of him, is forced into retirement after injury and a run of losses. Against the backdrop of America's Great Depression, he is forced to wait at the docks each morning, queuing up with the many unemployed men. He hopes to be picked for a day's labour so that he is not reduced to begging. The family face the hardships of having their electricity disconnected, diluting milk so there is enough to go round, and watching their children get ill from poor nutrition. Jim is given another chance in the ring, and takes on a major fight even though he is inadequately prepared and his opponent is on top form. As Braddock takes punch after punch it is a vision of his starving children that keeps him going: he's fighting for them, risking his life to keep them fed.

When our children need us, all the best parts of our human nature kick in. This inbuilt compassion for our own is a mirror of God's heart for us. In the Revelation passage we are shown the intimate picture of God the Father taking the time to wipe away the tears from our eyes. Human beings are valuable to God. He choses to allow his Son to offer himself as a sacrifice. He choses not to rescue him from the cross, in order that he could rescue us from our sin. Our value as human beings is underwritten by the fact that God made us, that we belong to him, and that he has paid a great price to rescue us from the mess we have made of our lives and the planet.

No longer do we need to be protected from the white-hot holiness of God. He comes in close and comforts us. He removes the crying and the pain and bereavement and death. Finally, we have come home to a loving Father, to a perfect community. We have arrived where we were born to be. The human story is a journey from relationship with God, through rebellion and separation, through trusting Jesus for forgiveness, and back to relationship with God.

Escape to Victory

The England football team are a nightmare to support, as they continually seem to under-perform, or win only by the skin of their teeth. But once it was a different story. The 30th July 1966 was a day to remember. London's Wembley stadium was packed with 93,000 spectators, including the Queen and Prince Philip. England faced stiff opposition from West Germany, and after twelve minutes thirty-two seconds they were ahead. Now if you are an England fan this information does not disturb you, because you know that only four minutes later Geoff Hurst will equalize, then Martin Peters will score again in the seventy-eighth minute. The Germans equalize, forcing the game into extra time. But still you are not worried, because you know that in the ninety-eighth minute of play Geoff Hurst will strike again and then, right at the end of the game, those immortal words of Kenneth Wolstenholme: "Some people are on the pitch. They think it's all over." Then, as Geoff Hurst scores again, he says: "It is now!" Knowing how things end up helps us to weather the emotional ups and downs that come our way. Knowing the end result allows you to keep going when the chips are down.

Knowing how history ended up gave the Zimbabwean students courage to risk standing up for the truth. It enabled Christians in Rome to face the lions. It allowed Christians under persecution in the former Soviet Union to carry on meeting even if it meant being sent to the Gulag. It allows believers in North Korea to carry on serving God despite the concentration camps they are sent to if discovered.

Everyone knows we can't take it with us when we go, but we still play the game of life as if it were a game of Monopoly(tm) in which the person with the most property at the end wins. Knowing how the story ends helps us to decide what to invest our lives in. The vision of the future provided by the Christian faith resonates with our instincts that in the end relationships are what really matter, and doing all we can to use our resources to help others is the best use of what we've got.

Ever After

The four relationships we have looked at during the course of this book provide a structure for the fundamental elements of the Christian faith. We saw that originally God created a world where we lived in peace with him, ourselves, each other and the physical world. We had a clear identity and a clear purpose. We saw how breaking relationship with God had knock-on effects on all areas of life. We saw how these fractured relationships are part of our everyday experience and explain the frustrations we face. Yet we still see glimpses of how the world should have been when things are at their best. We saw how Jesus lived in peace in all these areas. He was unique in that he managed to live in this broken world and still maintain perfect relationships. We saw how Jesus' death on the cross provided a way for us to live in peace with our creator, our neighbours, our planet and ourselves. Finally, we see how history ends up. Perfect peace once more. At the end of time, we discover what God had originally planned for us in the first place, only better. We will experience the true understanding of significance, identity, community and destiny.

It was three o'clock in the morning and I was flying high above the Indian Ocean. I was fighting a battle against sleep. I had tried everything. I had dosed myself up with caffeine, I had pinched myself, slapped my cheeks and turned the ventilation on full. But I was fighting a losing battle. I was gripped by the inflight movie and was desperate to know what happened in the end. Would the hero save the world? Would the heroine meet the man of her dreams? Would justice finally be served? But it was no use. Sleep had a stronger grip and it was only in my dreams that I could begin to guess the ending. I woke up with the credits rolling. What had really happened? There was no way of finding out. The film was no longer on in the cinemas. The DVD was not out. I was left with that frustrated, dissatisfied feeling. I still wonder how on earth it ended. I remind myself that sometimes even when we do see the end of the movie we are not satisfied. Unresolved plot lines and loose ends leave us hanging. We like to know that there is a dramatic climax and a neat, happy-ever-after ending.

In this chapter, we have been able to press the fast-forward button to see that history really does have a happy ending. It is possible to literally live happily ever after. God, the hero of the story, rescues the world. The bride gets her husband and justice is well and truly served. We do not have to lose sleep worrying about how things will turn out in the end. But we do have a decision to make. The Bible does not promise this happy ending for everyone. It is offered freely to all of us, but not all of us will choose to accept it. The remote is in your hands. Only you can decide how you will respond to God's offer of peace.

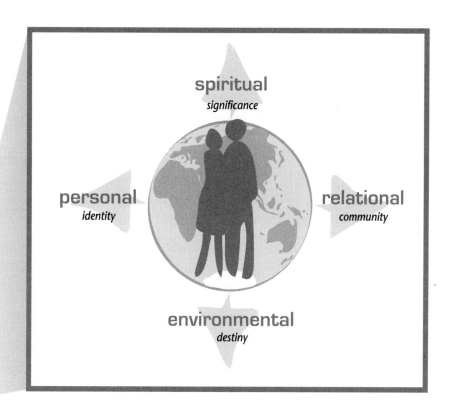

play

Thank you for taking time out with me to press pause on the DVD of life. Together we have looked at some of life's persistent questions. We have seen how the Christian faith provides a framework for life. It connects with the deepest longings of our hearts. It ties up many of the loose ends in our lives. This is a short book. These are big questions. There is plenty more that can be said. What will you do next? Will you allow life simply to play itself out? Or will you follow the clues we have been exploring together and begin to connect your plan with God's big story for the universe? The time has come for us to take our finger off the pause button on the remote. Before you press play, can I suggest some ways in which you might continue on your exploration?

On Your Knees:

Here is a prayer you might find helpful as you continue your search:

Dear God

I want to know more about you and start to get to know you personally. Help me to follow the clues I see in my life that will lead me to you. Help me accept your way to live in peace with you, other people, the world and myself. Help me to discover my true destiny.

Amen.

On the Web:

www.bethinking.org
www.rzim.org
www.rejesus.org
www.findachurch.co.uk

On the bookshelf:

The Bible.
Lewis, C.S. Mere Christianity, Collins, 1998.
Wright, Tom. Simply Christian, SPCK Publishing, 2006.
Zacharias, Ravi. Can Man Live Without God? Word Publishing, 1994.

Down the street:

There is a very user-friendly course that has been developed for people who want to continue investigating the Christian faith. The Alpha Course has helped many thousands of people around the world to take a closer look at the claims of the Bible. Log onto www.alpha.org to find a local church that is running a course near you.

On DVD:

Chariots of Fire (1981), directed by Hugh Hudson.
Shadowlands (1993), directed by Richard Attenborough.
The Passion of the Christ (2004), directed by Mel Gibson.
The Chronicles of Narnia: The Lion, The Witch and The Wardrobe
(2005), directed by Andrew Adamson.

References

1 The Bourne Identity (2002) directed by Doug Liman.

2 To see the lizard-man, check out http://www.bmeworld.com/amago/

3 Jones, D. (2005) iPod, Therefore I Am, Orion Books.

4 Kabat-Zinn, J. (2005) Wherever You Go, There You Are: Mindfulness Meditation in Everyday Life, Hyperion.

5 Russell, B. (1968) The Autobiography of Bertrand Russell, Vol. 2, Little Brown & Co., pp. 95-96.

6 Lewis, C.S. (1952) Mere Christianity, Macmillan, p. 105.

7 Blocher, Henri (1984) In the Beginning, Leicester: IVP.

8 Dead Poets Society (1989) directed by Peter Weir.

9 Thoreau, H.D. (1854) Walden, Ticknor and Field.

10 Parsons, R. (1995) The Sixty-Minute Father, Hodder & Stoughton, pp. 17-18.

11 Lewis, C.S. (1976) Mere Christianity, Fontana, p.118.

12 Ravi Zacharias, cite with reference to *Who God Created Us to Be*

13 Solzhenitsyn, A. (1973) The Gulag Archipelago, Harper & Row, p. 168.

14 Coupland, D. (1994) Life After God, Scribner, p. 250.

15 John 1:29.

16 Matthew 5:9.

17 Brown, Lindsay (2006) *Shining Like Stars*, IVP, p. 123

References to picture quotations

p.15. Jones, D.(2005) *IPod, Therefore I Am*, Orion Books

p.38 Pascal, B. (1995) *Pensees*, Penguin Books, p.181

p.47 Chesterton, G.K. (1963), *Orthodoxy*, Fontana, p.53

p.66. Camus, A. (2005) *The Myth of Sisyphus*, Penguin Books

p.93 Assayas, M (2006) *Bono on Bono: Conversations with Michka Assayas*, Hodder, p205

p.123 Pascal, B. (1995) *Pensees*, Penguin Books, p.47

Photo credits:

Jonathan Self: Pages 17, 20, 43, 47, 56, 62, 65, 80, 105, 110, 126
For more information on Jonathan Self's photographs, or for private commissions and sales, please contact him on jonself@hotmail.com

Roger Chouler: Page 15

Estelle Lobban: Pages 33, 37, 93, 123 plus Notes Background

Julia Mosca: Page 85

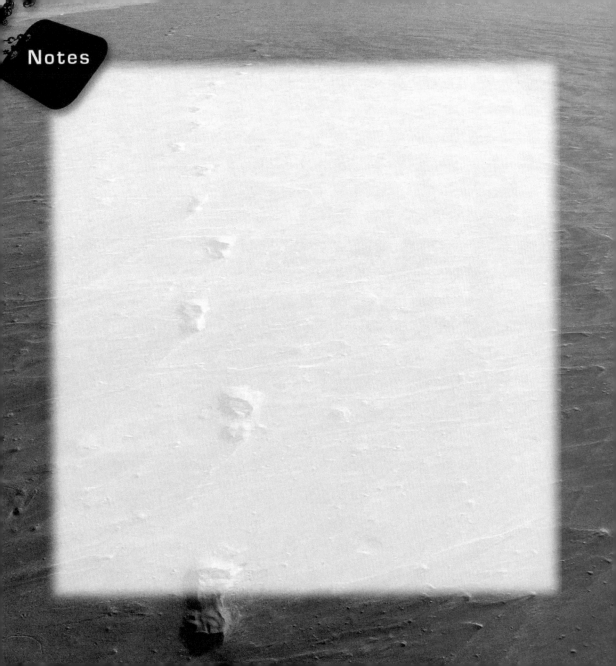